# HOW TO START
# YOUR OWN BUSINESS
# WITHOUT LOSING
# YOUR SHIRT

ARTHUR MORTIMER LEVITT *with his wife, Mimi, on the street where they live.*

# How to Start
# Your Own Business
# Without Losing
# Your Shirt

■ □ ■

## SECRETS OF
## SEVENTEEN SUCCESSFUL
## ENTREPRENEURS

■ □ ■

## Mortimer Levitt

*New York   ATHENEUM   1988*

OTHER BOOKS BY MORTIMER LEVITT

*Class: What It Is and How to
Acquire It   1984*

*The Executive Look: How to Get
It—How to Keep It   1981*

Atheneum
Macmillan Publishing Company
866 Third Avenue, New York, N.Y. 10022
Collier Macmillan Canada, Inc.

Library of Congress Cataloging-in-Publication Data
Levitt, Mortimer, ──────
  How to start your own business without losing your shirt :
secrets of seventeen successful entrepreneurs /
Mortimer Levitt.
    p.  cm.
  ISBN 0-689-11958-5
  1. New business enterprises—Case studies.  2. Entrepre-
neurship—Case studies.  I. Title.
HD62.5.L48   1988
658.1'141—dc19   88-15318   CIP

■ □ ■

This book is dedicated to four men and one woman, each of whom helped shape The Custom Shop as it stands today:

Jules Seiden, 1939 to present, Senior Vice President, Display and New Store Construction.

Christian Gagnaire, 1949 until his death in May 1988, Plant Manager.

Estelle Rubenstein, 1940 to present, Financial Adviser.

Glenn Bernbaum, 1959 to 1979, Executive Vice President and Chief Operating Officer.

Anthony Bergamo, 1979 to present, President and Chief Operating Officer.

# Acknowledgments

It was a wise man who said, "No man stands alone"—least of all this one. And I am most fortunate to still have with me Katie Rawdon, whose cheerful willingness to take everything down and keep it all in order made writing this book relatively easy. And thanks, also, to Betty Vaughn, Custom Shop's public relations consultant, whose persistence finally persuaded me to sit down and write it. And, of course, the manuscript might not have been finished if my wife, Mimi, had not given me moral support.

# Contents

"All I want is a country where every man
can get rich."

RONALD REAGAN

☐

"Success in business is not for the greedy—
on the contrary; success results from
giving more without charging more, and
the possibilities are infinite."

MORTIMER LEVITT

# 1
■ □ ■

# How to Start Your Own Business Without Losing Your Shirt

**E** ndless trouble is the price we all must pay for the gift of life, and starting your own business will surely increase your troubles substantially.

Yet starting your own business—and perhaps even becoming a millionaire—is the American Dream, a valid dream that is, happily, alive and well. And if we think about it at all, we Americans really are privileged; becoming a millionaire cannot be, for instance, the Soviet Dream—at least, not as of this writing.

The early 1980s were the most entrepreneurial years in American history. In 1983, some 700,000 new businesses were started. About 80 percent of them have failed or will fail, but that's not the point. What's clear is that an increasing number of Americans want a piece of their own action. And President Reagan gave them additional encouragement when he announced his new tax proposals in 1985: "Why not set out with your friends on the path to adventure and start your own business? You, too, can become leaders in this great new era of progress—the age of the entrepreneur."

By starting your own business, I don't mean a business like the typical mom-and-pop store—a dry cleaner's, a stationery store, a hardware store, etc. That kind of "going into business" is simply an alternative way of making a living. In some ways, it is more desirable—*you* are the boss. In some ways, it is less desirable, because you work much, much harder. And the income usually is no more than you might earn in a middle-management position.

I wrote this book for three reasons:

1. Starting your own business is relatively easy, but keeping it solvent is *not* easy. The dismal statistic that *four out of five new businesses fail* suggests that certain would-be entrepreneurs would do better by *not* plunging blindly ahead, so my book may actually act as a deterrent, in which case you can be sure of keeping possession of your shirt. My case studies will alert you to the many hazards that in one way or another befall most entrepreneurs. But, and more importantly, they will also act as a guide, a box score, or a level for comparison against which you can measure your contemplated project, your own skills, and your personal aptitudes. I hope the success stories that make up this book will offer encouragement to those ambitious individualists who decide to go ahead, because the stories make clear that the opportunities are endless for those who are deadly serious about owning a business.

2. For today's would-be entrepreneur, there appears to be little realistic information available in published form. Books such as *In Search of Excellence*, and its more-of-the-same sequel, *A Passion for Excellence*, have been blockbuster best-sellers but offer little practical value.

After reading both books carefully, I made no changes in the way I operate my business. To put it another way, I read 750 pages and learned little or nothing. My chief operating officer, Anthony Bergamo, also read them and came to the same conclusion quite independently.

To make certain that Anthony and I were not the exception, I asked several friends for their opinions. Five top executives agreed with us but didn't want to be quoted. Yet the fact that both books became outstanding best-sellers was a clear indication of a need still unfulfilled.

3. The personal entrepreneurial success I've been fortunate enough to enjoy as the sole owner of The Custom Shop, Shirtmakers/Tailors has provoked considerable curiosity among friends, acquaintances, and the tens of thousands of Custom Shop customers who have expressed their admiration for our operation. So it occurred to me that the inside story of my business, warts and all, would be of more than passing interest to anyone contemplating a new venture.

The authors of the "Excellence" books are professional corporate consultants. Consultants tell those whose businesses are not doing well what is wrong, and suggest ways to fix them. However, they don't stay around long enough to do the job themselves. And there is an enormous difference between telling someone how to do something and actually *doing* it. The fact that the consulting business consists of consultants acting as "kibitzers" rather than players might indicate that sometime, somewhere, the same consultants may have failed as players, or indeed, never played the game at all. And their fees may seem to be unconscionable. A consultant who earns a $75,000 salary is usually billed at three and one-half times his base salary to cover his base and benefits, hours not billed, and the consulting firm's overhead and profit. So you pay the price of a two-star general, but all you get is a lieutenant.

Here is a small example of the kind of double talk that consultants are capable of. Robert H. Waterman, who coauthored *In Search of Excellence*, was interviewed by the *New York Times* in March 1987. The subject is corporate renewal, how corporations that were in trouble (Ford, Olivetti, Maytag, et al.) brought themselves back to life:

**Q:** To what extent do they owe their nine lives to an ability to plan for the future?

**A:** They realize that the future is unpredictable. So the least important thing to come out of the planning process as far as many of these companies are concerned is the plan itself. Indeed, their major strategies are often opportunistic.

Rather, they use the planning process as an internal communications device. And more important than the plan itself is the information the process generates on markets and competitors, which helps them identify potential crises and opportunities. I.B.M. uses its planning process to integrate the way its many divisions serve a given customer. Wells Fargo's enabled it to recognize and seize a major opportunity and buy Crocker when it was suddenly offered up for sale.

I object to Mr. Waterman's statements, "the least important thing . . . is the plan itself. . . . Indeed, their major strategies are often opportunistic." This entire paragraph is a form of business Jabberwocky. He has borrowed certain popular catch phrases, and analyzed nothing. He has given his readers no insight into what went into the turnaround at Ford, Olivetti, and Maytag.

Instead of analyzing Fortune 500 corporations, I have profiled smaller businesses that were both successful and unique. It is the *conception* of a new idea for a business *and the successful execution* of that idea to which this book will address itself. Conception and execution in the early stages will be studied microscopically to discover the one or two *basic concepts* that led to the successful results.

One tiny example of the importance of concept: Dr. George Gallup built his enormously successful polling organization on one small insight, and like most simple ideas one wonders why it wasn't obvious to everyone at the time.

In the 1936 presidential election, *Literary Digest* (the *Time* magazine of its day) predicted the victory of Alf Landon over FDR by nineteen points. Gallup was suspicious of a prediction relying on telephone interviews, for in 1936, telephones were confined mostly to *upper-income* homes. Gallup polled a more representative sample of the population, and successfully predicted the reelection of Roosevelt. The result was oblivion for *Literary Digest*, world-wide fame for Gallup.

My book is *not* intended to be an encyclopedia of get-rich-quick schemes. Rather, there are examples of seventeen businesses that started, seemingly from nowhere, from an idea, a concept, a "What if?" and went on to achieve a substantial success, in most cases *without* going public. The variety spans a wide range:

- a computerized real-estate business
- a snob-appeal restaurant
- a family clothing store
- an innovative postcardiac health-care facility
- a unique salvage company
- an incredible pharmaceutical marketing ploy
- a one-of-a-kind food market grossing $80 million a year
- a smorgasbord of marketing and advertising services grossing $400 million

Each business is explored from the very beginning—the concept and the jelling of that concept, up to and including the decision "I'll do it!" And then, of course, how the business was nursed through its beginning stages—that most crucial time, including the initial blunders, misconceptions, and finally that devilish X factor—the single, totally unexpected situation that no research can uncover, because it happens *after* the fact.

I spent most of my time searching out these smaller companies because my readers are not likely to start another General Motors, and therefore, I hope, will find my stories of greater relevance. The United States' free-flowing capitalism offers endless opportunities to start your own business. And small businesses can be extremely profitable. For an entrepreneur to clear a million or two, pretax, in a business of modest size, is not unusual. In contrast, there are very few chief executive officers of even the country's large corporations who earn that kind of money. So, contrary to the advice of my friends, I am placing my *emphasis* on what I think of as "sleepers"—small idea businesses that produce considerable income for the individual owner, and, as an extra, special bonus, supply the entrepreneur with the ego satisfaction that all humans need and want.

As you read about the entrepreneurs I have included, you will realize that there are *no* hard and fast rules for going into business. But the stories will give you important insights, insights I wish I had had when I started The Custom Shops.

Incidentally, I made it a point *not* to ask the entrepreneurs who confided in me what their pretax profits are, although in some cases they volunteered the information. Unlike public companies, an entrepreneur's balance sheet is shown only to his or her banker and the Internal Revenue Service, and that, perhaps, is how it should be.

## THE ONE IMPORTANT QUESTION
## THAT YOU MUST ANSWER

When an entrepreneur starts a business, it is frequently the result of a need personally observed. The Custom Shop had its inception, as you will discover, in my neck: my neck was skinny, but my shoulders were broad, so if a ready-to-wear shirt fit my shoulders, its collar was too large, and if the collar was correct, the shoulders were too narrow. Julian Brodie's consulting service on the problems of retirement originated with his struggle to ease life for his own aging parents. Stew Leonard's broad-based retail success grew out of a keenly felt personal need to make something of value from his father's failing milkman's routes. Julee Rosso and Sheila Lukins were stimulated to open The Silver Palate by perceiving in their own hectic daily schedules the need many women had for a resource to help them entertain in style, but without cooking, at the end of a day. We all had an answer to that most important question: *Why should customers come to me for their goods/service/whatever, instead of continuing to go where they have been going!* I would suggest that you do not open your new business unless you have studied that question seriously and have come up with a serious answer.

Nevertheless, I have also included a few entrepreneurs who started their businesses *without* being able to answer that key question positively. Glenn Bernbaum, who owns Mortimer's, simply asked, "Why should I drink at someone else's bar when I can drink at my own?" Arthur Imperatore had no education and no money, but his four older brothers owned two underutilized Army surplus trucks. Gene Ballin agreed to build a house for a flat fee, saving his customer the usual 15 percent overhead and 10 percent profit tacked on by all contractors. Kenny Lane accidentally stumbled onto a need. Bill Raveis was determined never again to work for anybody because of one unhappy experience as an employee. He looked around and chose the thing closest at hand, which happened to be real estate. George Lindemann bought three pharmaceutical companies and only *then* proceeded to search out a marketable product.

Each one of these dare-takers latched onto an angle well *after* he started his business. So there is no single right or wrong scenario to explain why some of these entrepreneurs have succeeded. Their stories are laid out here as a kind of spectrum of business experience to give you an opportunity to select the particular points to which you can personally relate. One man's aptitude is another man's poison. Some of the bungled experiences exposed here may help you decide *not* to start your own business.

## YOUR COMPETITION

Anyone who contemplates going into business should be made aware of the caliber of competition that he or she will run into, and the enormous effort that strong-willed individuals will make to leave their mark. For example, take my friend Samuel LeFrak, whose biography I reprint below in its five-point entirety from the 1987–1988 edition of *Who's Who in the World.*

Sam LeFrak's story is not detailed in this book, because I am not sure you would learn anything from it. Briefly, he has built more apartments in New York City than any other builder. He is New York City's largest taxpayer. He helped design and build Battery Park City on 340 acres of land dredged out of the Hudson River. And now he is building Newport in New Jersey, on the banks of the Hudson, directly across from Battery Park City—a huge development

**LEFRAK, SAMUEL J.**, housing and bldg. corp. exec., real estate devel., fin., oil and gas exploration, communications, music-pub., motion picture exec., pub. ofcl.; b. N.Y.C., Feb. 12, 1918; s. Harry and Sarah (Schwartz) L.; grad. U. Md., 1940; postgrad. Columbia, Harvard; Sc.D., London Coll. Applied Sci., 1970; LL.D., N.Y. Law Sch., 1975, Colgate U., 1979; consulate laureate Univ. Studies, Rome, 1972; m. Ethel Stone, May 14, 1941; children—Denise, Richard, Francine, Jacqueline. Pres., Lefrak Orgn., 1948—, chmn. bd., 1975—; developer Battery Park City, 1985; creator, sponsor, builder Lefrak City; developer Newport City, 1985—; mem. adv. bd. Sta. WHLI, 1955; commr. Landmarks Preservation Commn. N.Y.C., 1966; commr. pub. works Borough Manhattan, 1956-58; commr. Interstate Sanitation Commn., 1958; Saratoga Springs Commn., 1962—. Mem. adv. bd. Chem Bank.; guest lectr. Harvard Grad. Sch. Bus. Adminstrn., 1971, Yale, 1975, N.Y. U., 1977; guest speaker Financial Women's Assn. N.Y., 1975; guest lectr. Princeton U., 1983, U. Haifa, 1983, Oxford U., 1984, others; featured speaker Instl. Investment Real Estate Conf., 1975; U.S. del. Internat. Conf. Housing and Urban Devel., Switzerland, 1967; dir. N.Y. World's Fair Corp., 1964-65, N.Y. Indsl. Devel. Corp., 1975—; chmn. bd. L.I. Post; pres. N.Y.C. Comml. Devel. Corp., 1967-71, chmn., 1971—; founding mem. World Business Council, Inc., 1970; mem. Gov. N.Y. finance and adv. com. N.Y. State Traffic Safety Council, 1966; mem. Pres.'s Com. Employment Handicapped; spl. cons. urban affairs State Dept., 1969; mem. adv. council Real Estate Inst., N.Y. U., 1970—; commr. Saratoga-Capital dist. N.Y. State Park and Recreation Commn., 1973; mem. N.Y.C. Pub. Devel. Corp.; mem. Nat. Energy Council, U.S. Dept. Commerce; mem. Mayor's Com. on Housing Devel., N.Y.C., 1974—; mem. exec. com. Citizen's Com. for N.Y.C., Inc., 1975—; mem. N.Y. State Gov.'s Task Force on Housing, 1974, vice chmn.-at-large A.R.C. in N.Y.; mem. U.S. com. UN Orgn., 1957; chmn. nat. bd. Histadrut, 1967—; chmn. bldg. com. Saratoga Performing Arts; mem. Fifth Ave. Assn.; dir., chmn. real estate div. Greater N.Y. Fund; hon. com. A.A.U.; Queens chmn. United Greek Orthodox Charities, 1973; chmn. Celebrity Sports Night-Human Resources Center, 1973-74; trustee, dir. Beth-El Hosp.; bd. dirs. U.S.O., Citizens Housing and Planning Council N.Y., 1957—, Interfaith Movement, Diabetics Found., Queens Cultural Assn., Consumer Credit Counseling Service Greater N.Y., Astoria Motion Picture and TV Center Found.; trustee N.Y. Law Sch., Queens Art and Cultural Center, N.Y. Citizens Budget Com., Jewish Hosp. at Denver, Brookdale Hosp. Med. Center; trustee, mem. adv. bd. Pace U.; mem. exec. bd. Greater N.Y. councils Boy Scouts Am.; founder Albert Einstein Sch. Medicine; bd. govs. Invest-in-Am. Nat. Council; mem. task force on energy conservation Div. Housing and Community Renewal, 1981—; mem. nat. com. Scandinavia Today, 1981—. Decorated Order St. John of Jerusalem (Pope John); Order of Lion of Finland; recipient Mayor N.Y.C. award outstanding citizenship, 1960; Nat. Boys Club award, 1960; Citizen of Year award B'nai B'rith, 1963, Distinguished Achievement award, 1967; Man of Year award V.F.W., 1963; Brotherhood award NCCJ, 1964; Chief Rabbi Herzog gold medal, Torah Fellowship citation Religious Zionist Am., 1966; John F. Kennedy Peace award, 1966; Man of Year award Bklyn. Community Hosp., 1967; Builder of Excellence award Brandeis Sch., 1968; Master Builder award N.Y. Cardiac Center, 1968; Distinguished Citizen award M Club Found. U. Md., 1970; Distinguished Alumnus award U. Md. Alumni Assn., 1970; Am. Eagle award nat. council Invest-in Am., 1972; Exec. Sportsman award Human Resources Center, 1973; Archtl. award Fifth Ave. Assn., 1974; Excellence in Design award Queens C. of C., 1974; Am. Achievement award, 1984; named hon. citizen Md., 1970. Mem. Sales Execs. Club N.Y. (dir.), United Hunts Racing Assn., Philharmonic Symphony Soc. N.Y., Explorers Club (dir.), Phi Kappa Phi, Tau Epsilon Phi (established Samuel J. LeFrak scholarship award 1975). Clubs: Masons, Shriners; Lotos (dir. 1975—, Merit award 1973), Grand Street Boys, Friars (dir. Found.), Advertising, Economic, Downtown Athletic (N.Y.C.); Town; Turf and Field; Cat Cay (Nassau, Bahamas); Xanadu Yacht (Freeport, Grand Bahamas); Palm Bay (Miami Beach, Fla.); Seawane; Ocean Reef (Key Largo); Sag Harbor Yacht (L.I.). Office: 97-77 Queens Blvd Forest Hills NY 11374 on 250 acres. Plans call for four high-rise residential towers with 1,500 apartments, a 1.5-million-square-foot regional shopping center, an elevated roadway and secondary roads, and a huge new sewer system, etc., etc.

His *Who's Who* profile also reveals his many activities *outside* of business. The man's energy is staggering. There are other business people with only a fraction of that energy who are nonetheless potential formidable competitors in your own field. *Remember*: Capitalism is strictly for players of hardball.

## WHO WILL SUCCEED?

> *Success in business is not for the greedy—*
> *on the contrary; success results from giving*
> *more without charging more, and the pos-*
> *sibilities are infinite.*

The quote is mine, and you will find it in the biography under my name in *Who's Who in America*.

Some people realize their potential after they choose the life of an entrepreneur. I know I did. Whatever talents I may have had while a salaried salesman were lying dormant until I started The Custom Shop. That initial achievement inspired an effort to achieve even more. "Success," someone once wrote, "breeds success."

There are, of course, many reasons for failure, among them the most popular excuse, undercapitalization. Then there are personality characteristics that may turn an entrepreneur's success into a rapid failure: an inclination to gamble, an inability to delegate authority, an unwillingness to listen to the opinion of others, perhaps a failure to attract and nurture managerial talent, or a failure to monitor changing trends.

In my opinion, however, most new businesses fail because they have no substantive answer to that one important question: *Why should customers come to me for their goods/ service/whatever, instead of continuing to go where they have been going?*

Yet a positive response to that big question is not the only requirement for success. That question is only the beginning, and surely it must be backed with *motivation* that is *above and beyond the norm*. It should be obsessive. Then, too, one must think in terms of a *complete* package: presentation, service, product, finance, timing, and finally, execution. To all of that, unfortunately, must be added the aforementioned X factor, that unknown future intrusion from new legislation, economic depression, confiscation by a foreign government, overproduction in the market, a new competitor with an improved idea, and of course, happenstance—luck—sometimes good, sometimes bad.

Nor can personal aptitudes be underestimated as a factor for success. Men like John McEnroe, Sir Laurence Olivier, and Lee Iacocca are not just the result of training. They are extraordinarily gifted. If 100 on an I.Q. test is average, these three men would score 160 in the area of their special aptitudes.

Let's take a brief look at Iacocca, the miracle man. His success in turning the Chrysler Corporation around from near bankruptcy seems to have turned on the whole country. In essence, the seemingly complicated story of his extraordinary success is simple.

The United States was almost unanimous in giving the raspberry to Charles E. Wilson (president of General Motors from 1941 to 1953). In 1953, he put his foot in his mouth during the Senate confirmation hearings on his appointment as secretary of defense when he said, "I honestly believe that what is good for America is good for General

Motors, and vice versa." But Wilson was prescient considering the Chrysler situation. Many years later, when Iacocca went to the U.S. government and said, "If Chrysler goes under, it will be bad for America," the government came through; it did *not* give him the raspberry. But then, having received the necessary funds to avoid bankruptcy, how did Iacocca turn that troubled company around?

Well, for starters, Iacocca took to the airwaves promoting Chrysler's original reason for existence: their *engineering* expertise. He parlayed the company's excellent reputation in this area by adding his personal expertise as an engineer for Ford. And Iacocca backed that up with a five-year/50,000-mile guarantee on every new automobile sold. Iacocca stuck his neck out. He went on television *personally* and said, in effect, "I guarantee it," and he said "Chrysler has always been the engineering leader of the industry, and that's what I am—an engineer." It was no secret that the wildly successful Ford Mustang had been Iacocca's baby, and that helped him, too.

Iacocca had one more thing: credibility. His personal, down-to-earth approach on television gave credibility to his claims and to his product guarantees.

In contrast, that other would-be automaker, John De-Lorean, failed miserably under similar circumstances. Like Iacocca, DeLorean also gained government funding, in British sterling, not dollars, for a manufacturing plant in Northern Ireland, but he was unable to deliver on any of his promises. Incidentally, in one of DeLorean's early efforts to raise money in the United States, I was one of a small group of potential investors invited to lunch at New York's elegant St. Regis Hotel. After lunch, DeLorean made a slide presentation showing the projected profits for the company producing his dynamic new sports car. I remember whispering to a friend, "There's no way I would trust this man with any of *my* money." To me at least, DeLorean had no credibility. His shirt collar was too flamboyant! As it turned out, so was his lifestyle.

If there is a single common element in the lives of the seventeen entrepreneurs profiled in this book, it is unrelenting motivation. In various ways, these men and women exhibit the kind of drive—an all-encompassing determination and concentration on getting ahead—call it what you will. It also builds careers in the arts, sports, and politics. It is a will to shine, not merely survive.

The fact is, apart from those few individuals who enjoy the mixed blessing of inherited wealth, no one rises in business without breathing hard. Talent, like the heart muscle, diminishes without steady exercise. A new idea withers and dies without forceful promotion and execution. Energy and concentration, and then still more energy, is required to bring about a result in the marketplace that inertia and chance naturally conspire to prevent. Ignore my own seemingly languid example—I retired from the day-to-day operations in 1941, four years after I started The Custom Shop. There is no such thing as a nine-to-five entrepreneur. Be prepared to throw yourself behind your idea to the exclusion of almost everything else—sports, cultural events, and even family. Success demands *more* than a good idea. It demands fanatical devotion.

If you cannot extrapolate anything from the stories that follow, if you cannot find inspiration, or at the very least, practical ideas for your personal needs, then perhaps you are better off not starting your own business.

So let's begin the quest with the complete story of my beloved Custom Shops, a business with which I have been intimately acquainted for the past fifty years.

MORTIMER LEVITT, *founder and owner, The Custom Shop, Shirtmakers/Tailors*

# 2

∎ □ ∎

# The Custom Shop's Preposterous Beginnings

Fifty years after its modest opening, The Custom Shop has eighty-one stores, coast-to-coast. I am still the sole owner—no partners, no stockholders, no franchises, and, believe it or not, no competitors. Now I don't mean there are no other shirtmakers. There are. But a shirtmaker who gets 30 percent more for a shirt identical to mine (cut and sewn in The Custom Shop way) cannot be considered a competitor.

But perhaps I should begin at the beginning. I was born and raised in indifferent circumstances in Brooklyn. I became a high school dropout at the beginning of my third year at Boys High School, having flunked first-term Latin twice, first-term French twice, and first-term Spanish once. I knew no one who spoke Latin, French, or Spanish. I lived in the heart of Brooklyn, and saw no reason why I should spend my time conjugating verbs I had no occasion to use.

The school *insisted* that a student must qualify in a foreign language to graduate, but I had the last word: I just dropped out.

There was also another reason. My father was unemployed, and my two brothers were too young to work. The family needed whatever income I could produce, which as an office boy at J. W. Davis & Company, Stockbrokers, was sixteen dollars for a five-and-a-half-day work week. It all went to my mother (it was 1923 and there was no income tax, at least in my bracket), who in turn gave me fifty cents a day. Subway fare was a nickel, and Mother packed my lunch, leaving forty cents a day to do with as I wished.

Unhappy in the Wall Street environment because of its mindless anti-Semitism, I looked for and found a similar position at Erlanger, Blumgart, converters of fine cotton fabrics for ladies' sports dresses. It was January 1924. Erlanger was the first United States converter to offer cotton fabrics that did not fade, made possible through a new dyeing process invented in Germany. In 1923, their Everfast name was already well known. Two years later, I was promoted to salesman. I was a relatively successful salesman for the first two years. Then I lost *all* motivation because I lost respect for my role model, David Sulzberger, a partner in the firm and New York sales manager. However, that's another story, the main point being that I was now completely indifferent to my job. Yet, privately, I knew I was not destined to live and die in Brooklyn.

I did love clothes, had a real feeling for them, as well as a strong and separate aptitude for doing anything and everything the easiest possible way—meaning, as a salesman, that I searched out and paid attention only to large accounts. The half-dozen large accounts I uncovered provided me with a relatively good income (in 1986 dollars, the equivalent of

$35,000) and left time for frequent matinees at the theater, or the movies. Wednesday matinee dancing at the Roseland Ballroom was an alternative, and there were always extended lunch hours with friends. This immature routine led to the inevitable. After thirteen years and half a dozen warnings, I was (and properly so) fired.

Ameritex, Everfast's chief competitor, was happy to take me on, providing I promised to change my errant ways. I was twenty-nine when I married my first wife, Anna Friede, an activist leftist and a beginning dress designer. I should have been concerned about issues like a job and financial security, but I wasn't. So things did not go well for me at Ameritex either. I really was *not* motivated and had even begun to lose my self-respect. Realizing that I was drifting, I wondered if there was something I could or should do on my own, and one day my thoughts wandered back to Mermelstein. I did have a skinny neck, and though this bit of anatomical news might not strike the reader as earth-shattering, it was, in fact, a skinny neck that indirectly launched my career as a shirtmaker. I wore a size 15 collar, but the shirt was too tight in the chest and shoulders. A 15 1/2 shirt would fit properly through the chest and shoulders but it would be too big in the neck. As a result, I had become a customer of Mermelstein. This refugee from Czarist Russia had a tiny business making shirts to order from the customers' own material, and I became one of his regulars. He charged $1.25 for "cut, make, and trim" (buttons, interlining, stays, and packaging). His shirts were produced in a small loft on the Lower East Side. He employed about nine sewing-machine operators. Mermelstein cut the shirts himself, and his son did the selling by making the rounds of the various cotton-goods houses on Worth Street.

Worth Street, in lower Manhattan, was in those days a center for the converters. It was their business to convert greige goods (raw fabric), into finished fabrics. The converters sold to manufacturers of dresses, shirts, ladies sportswear, children's dresses, and so on. Most customers bought sample cuttings before placing large orders, and other sample cuttings frequently found their way into the hands of employees in the sample room. That modest bit of chicanery, commonplace to the trade in those precomputer days, served as the raison d'être for Mermelstein's business.

## THE CONCEPT

One day, it was April 1937, I made a calculation—on my fingers, actually. If Mermelstein charged me $1.25 for a shirt, his total cost (labor, rent, trim, overhead, etc.) was probably 75 cents. It took three yards to make a shirt, and in those days the converters' price for domestic shirtings was 18 cents a yard. It seemed to me that I could make a shirt for about $1.30 (54 cents for material—75 cents for labor and overhead) and retail it profitably at $2.00. Arrow shirts were $1.85; my shirts would be *custom-made at almost the same price as ready-mades*, and there would be *no* inventory risk. Wow!

In 1937, custom-made shirts cost $6.00 for domestic cotton and up to $20.00 for Sea Island cotton, the very best. The idea of selling custom-made shirts at less than half the price of the "upstairs" shirtmakers seemed too good to be true, and the more I thought about it, the more excited I became. *There* was motivation! I was certainly not a shirtmaker, had never even worked in a retail store; nor had I ever been inside a shirt factory, but I knew, intuitively, that with my sense of style (I was always known as a "dresser") I could do a better job than Mermelstein, a Lower East Side "mechanic." I really couldn't think of Mermelstein as a shirtmaker; he had no sense of style whatsoever.

My thinking gradually unfolded as follows:

1. All shirtmakers bought their shirtings from jobbers—at retail. The jobbers would sell cuts of fifteen or thirty yards (even three yards), depending on a shirtmaker's needs. I took a calculated risk and went directly to the fabric mills and placed orders for full pieces. The mills gave me a hard time. They wanted me to buy from their customers, the jobbers. I explained that although I was opening only one store and one factory, it was my intention to open thirty-five stores, the first store being only a pilot. If the basic idea was sound, then there would be a need for a Custom Shop in every major city, and a city like New York could support five Custom Shops. Two mills finally agreed to sell me shirtings at factory-level prices, so I was able to effect an immediate savings of 40 percent on the fabric cost—a splendid competitive edge that was denied other shirtmakers.

2. I would require a minimum order of three shirts instead of the customary one shirt. This would lower both my cutting costs and my administrative costs substantially. At the same time, it would immediately increase my start-up volume.

3. My business would be strictly cash and carry—there would be no credit losses.

4. To be cost-efficient, my production system demanded a minimum of two thousand shirts a week. A chain of Custom Shops would easily give me the necessary volume. Until then, I would limp along as best I could.

5. I could afford to open stores in *prime* locations. The rent would be low, since I needed only a *tiny* space,

there being no inventory. All other shirtmakers were *upstairs*, as they needed to have their workrooms on the premises. My workrooms would be in a low-rent loft.

6. I would open my own factory right from the beginning, rather than trying to work with a contractor. Thus, I would save the contractor's profit and also pass that savings on to my customers. The entire process would become my personal secret. And there was absolutely no doubt in my mind that I could learn Mermelstein's process and *improve* on it, even though I had no idea at the time what his system was or exactly how I would do it better.

7. I would operate, in large measure, with my customers' money, as I would cut nothing without a substantial deposit.

But I did nothing about my new idea, except discuss it at some length with Mervin S. Levine, the custom tailor who had been making my suits for many years. He had misgivings. He said a retail price of $2.00 for a custom-made shirt was too low, that even if the shirts were good, people would not believe they *could* be good at that price. He said my minimum price should be $2.50; I compromised at $2.15.

I also talked about the idea with my wife and my wealthy in-laws (my mother-in-law had divorced and remarried, so by now I had two fathers-in-law). Despite my enthusiasm, their response was decidedly negative: they gave me no encouragement whatsoever. They just *knew* I didn't have what it took to be a businessman. I was thirty, and except for a handsome new wife who was well-born and well-bred, I was really without stature and seemingly without future. In addition to flunking out of high school, I had been fired from three of the only four jobs I had held.

At the end of June, despite all the negative advice, I decided to resign and go into business for myself. Was it possible that my secretly held high opinion of myself (that I was not destined to live and die in Brooklyn) was finally to be justified? I walked into my boss's office to tell him of my decision, but before I could do so, he told me, quite gently, that my services would no longer be required at Ameritex. Once again, I had followed my old pattern of coming in late, leaving early, and taking care only of large accounts. I was, and continue to be, a great simplifier, doing everything the easiest possible way. In any case, I had now been fired from four jobs out of four—obviously not an ideal background for starting a new business.

My entire savings at the time were invested in common stocks. In June my stocks were worth about $10,000. I had no need for the money until August. But in August 1937, there was a stock market crash that reduced my heavily margined account from $10,000 to $1,000. It was the third time I'd been cleaned out in the stock market: 1929, 1932, 1937.

Let's jump for just one moment ahead to June 1987. When the piano tuner finished tuning my piano, he asked if he might use my telephone. I said of course. Believe it or not, my piano tuner phoned his stockbroker to find out what the market did and how his stock, in particular, had fared. He earns about $40 an hour, but seldom puts in more than four hours a day. I told him to sell everything he had at once, but I could see from the wild look (gambling fever) in his eyes that he would do no such thing. I write this to give you some idea of the *lack* of knowledge that creates bull markets—a sixty-five-year-old piano tuner gambling away his life's earnings. (My advice: Stay out of the market. But if you *must* gamble, confine it to 20 percent, not more, of your capital.) Four months later, the stock market dropped

700 points. Incidentally, I followed my own advice having sold all my stock holdings in June of 1986.

I was so sure my new business would be successful, and so fearful that my "fabulous idea" would be copied, that I actually kept it a secret from the real-estate agent who rented me my first store. Nor did I tell the men who applied for the foreman's job exactly what I was doing either. (I placed a classified ad in the *New York Times*.) I told each applicant just enough to determine if I thought he could do the job. When I finally decided on the foreman I wanted, I took him into my confidence and had him show me how to take measurements. Since he had very little experience in custom-made shirts and I had none at all, it was another case (I'm sorry to say) of the blind leading the blind.

I borrowed $1,000 on my life-insurance policy, and with that and the $1,000 from my stocks, opened my first tiny Custom Shop along with a small factory fully stocked with nine sewing machines (rented) and a respectable inventory of shirt fabrics, collar linings, buttons, boxes, and order forms. My first store opened September 27, 1937. It was located at Broadway and Thirty-sixth Street, two blocks up from Macy's—at the time, one of New York's better shopping blocks. It was in the heart of the garment center, and there were plenty of fashion-conscious men on the streets. I needed a unique storefront, because my store was only seven feet wide inside, and my window only two and one-half feet wide by four feet deep. My original storefront (I applied for and received a design patent) was made of black Carrara glass, with a red-and-white-striped dome awning that called attention to the tiny window. The dome awning eventually became my logo and is actually better known than the name The Custom Shop, Shirtmakers.

The night prior to the opening, my wife sent me home

at 1 A.M., saying that I had to get some sleep if I was to open the next morning. I dreamed that my opening was so successful I had to call out the mounted police to keep people in line. So I was on a high when I reached my store the next morning at eight-fifteen. The window trimmer had finished his job. In the window, he had placed a hand-lettered sign bearing the first piece of advertising copy I had ever written:

### OUR STORY IS A SIMPLE ONE

We have devised a method whereby we can afford to custom-make shirts to your individual measurements with collar styles designed to complement your particular neck and face at $2.15, provided three or more shirts are ordered.

I thought the copy was splendid, and couldn't believe it came from me, because until then I had written nothing other than an occasional "Wish you were here" postcard.

At ten minutes to nine, I had just finished sweeping the floor when a man knocked on the door. I was hit with an acute attack of stage fright. I said, "Sorry, sir, we're not open yet, please come back at nine-thirty." Two minutes later, another man tried to open the door. I realized that if I was actually going to be in business for myself, I had *no choice*. I had to allow customers to come in. I put away my broom, turned on the lights, and opened the door.

After my first customer selected his shirtings, I took his measurements. Ten shirts hanging on the wall displayed various collar styles. (My beginnings were primitive; today each one of my designers has two hundred different collars that he can actually try on a customer.) When my customer selected the style he wanted, I realized that I had failed to mark the collars with names or pattern numbers. So, in the space indicated on the order for collar styles, I had to write, "Third collar from the right," etc. At the close of business that day, I removed the ten shirts from the wall and took them to my workrooms on Twenty-eighth Street along with my orders. But since I had neglected to keep the shirts in sequence, my improvised instructions became almost meaningless. My total lack of experience was beginning to show, but *my basic idea was so sound it made up for my inexperience.*

That first order for three shirts totaled $6.45, plus 13 cents sales tax (at that time a blessedly low 2 percent). I had decided to cut no shirt without a 25 percent deposit, so I proceeded to multiply $6.58 by 25 percent. In my confused state, this was beyond my ability (I might still find it difficult). Blushing furiously, I said, "Perhaps you'd better give me a three-dollar deposit." The customer said, "Fine," and handed me a ten-dollar bill. I hadn't known either that a retailer starts his day with cash in the drawer for making change. Actually, I had neither a cash drawer nor change. I suggested that he go to the cigar store in the lobby and get his bill changed. By then, my first customer must surely have had some misgivings, but he came back with the three dollars anyway.

Despite this rather ludicrous beginning, customers kept coming in. They came in off the street, attracted by the window display and by the extraordinarily low price. There were and there remains today a variety of sound reasons why a man might want to have shirts custom-made:

1. He has my problem—neck size and body size out of sync.
2. He has a favorite collar that is no longer in fashion.
3. He has a favorite fabric that he can't find ready-made.

4. His arms are extra long, or extra short, so he can't get his proper sleeve length in ready-made shirts.
5. Because of his height, he needs a tail length different than he can find in a ready-made shirt.
6. He wants a snug fit at the waist or needs much more room at the waist.
7. He wants to design his own collar style.
8. He needs a quarter-size collar (15 1/2 is too tight, 16 is too large; he needs 15 3/4).
9. He wants French cuffs or a two-button cuff rather than a one-button cuff.
10. One arm is longer than the other.
11. He has a paunch and can't button the bottom button of his ready-made shirt.
12. He likes the idea of having shirts custom-made.
13. He wants an oxford shirt but doesn't like button-down collars.

I knew that the quality of my shirts wouldn't be 100 percent at first, and they weren't, but I knew the fit would be much, much better than a man could get ready-made— and, of course, it was. It is not possible to start a new factory and get top quality, but I knew too that because New York was such a big city, the supply of new customers would be almost endless. As a concept, this turned out to be correct. New customers kept coming, and, of course, the shirts did get better. However, one disastrous day is still painfully etched in my memory.

I recall vividly an afternoon about three months after I opened. With six customers in the tiny store, it was filled to capacity. Two men wanted to order shirts and were looking at the fabrics. Another two were complaining. "You promised faithfully the shirts would be here by two forty-five. Where are they?" "These shirts were promised last week. Where are they?" A fifth man was saying, "Is this the way you think a custom shirt should fit?" And the sixth customer was pointing out that his shirts fit fine, but he knew he had never ordered a button-down collar. It is said that big trees from little acorns grow—but it would be surprising if anything other than a heart attack could grow out of a start like mine. Yet my basic concept was so sound, I had to be successful in spite of my shortcomings.

# 3

■ □ ■

# The Elements of Success

**P**rimarily, Custom Shop's success stemmed from my realization that the *only* extra money required for a custom-made shirt was the relatively modest extra cost of cutting a shirt individually (versus cutting them in bulk), *plus* the extra time required to take measurements and write up an order, which, in most cases, runs to about half an hour.

The thirty minutes of a designer's time (as opposed to the five minutes it takes a salesclerk to sell a ready-made shirt) was compensated for by my establishing prices based on cutting *three* shirts, not just one. And the extra cost for cutting shirts *individually* was covered by the fact that I was by-passing the manufacturer's profit. Too simple? Not at all. I was indeed a manufacturer, selling directly to the consumer through my own stores. This made it possible for our custom-made shirts to be priced the same as ready-made shirts of comparable quality.

Perhaps I should explain what was meant by "We have devised a method" in my window ad. It costs considerably more to cut shirts individually than it does to cut ready-made shirts that are piled a hundred high and then cut completely by machine or clicker. However, once the shirts are individually cut to the measurements taken by our designers, the big savings start. I "devised a method" whereby after the shirts are cut, they can then be sewn on a conveyor system, thus enabling the kind of savings Henry Ford effected when he developed the assembly line. I processed the thirty-one separate operations in the sewing of a shirt with a similar assembly-line concept. That's why I needed sales of at least two thousand shirts a week for a cost-efficient operation. "Upstairs" shirtmakers use one operator to sew the entire shirt, a setup that requires an extremely skilled operator—very hard to find, then or now—and, of course, much more costly, because it takes so much longer. Our operators, on the other hand, develop even more skill because each of them does only *one* operation. The key to getting quality in our system is having the proper number of inspections as the shirt moves down the line. Inspectors must make sure that each operation is done precisely.

That our inspection system paid off may be seen in the fact that less than 6 percent of our shirts are returned because of a fit problem. Some of those are due only to transposition errors in writing down or reading the original order. This in itself seems a minor miracle, taking into account that there are thirteen individual measurements (four on the collar and nine on the body) that must be written correctly, along with seven-digit fabric numbers.

I also developed a unique approach to designing collars, one that had never been used by other shirtmakers. Whereas collar styles were always designed by looking at the collar style from the front, we design collars by looking first at the *back*, since the height of the collar *in back* has to conform *to the length of the customer's neck*. To that end, we make every collar style in *five* different back heights and *four different* front heights.

However, that was only the concept. The rest of the package included a memorable logo—the striped-dome awning, which became immediately identifiable wherever it was seen, an elegant store design that features walnut walls, red velvet carpeting, indirect lighting, and in the opinion of many, incomparably well-designed shopfront windows. (This last feature is due entirely to the creative talents of Jules Seiden, who has been with me forty-seven years, and who also oversees the design and construction of all new stores.) The store design was intended to convey the feeling of elegance associated with "custom-made."

Then there were the additional unseen extras. From the start, I insisted that The Custom Shop was not in the shirt business but rather in a service business, a "make the customer look better" service. I believe we give this service in three ways:

1. By making shirts that compensate for any physical shortcomings.
2. By designing collars that are individually designed to complement a man's face and neck. (We treat the neck and face simply as two geometrical shapes.)
3. By educating a customer so that he projects an image consistent with his station in life. More on this later.

## MY EXPANSION PLAN

Adding shops was never based on any urgency to expand according to a business plan. Rather, new stores were opened whenever we found a location that seemed right, at a rent that was equitable. We also stayed within the parameters of the things we did best. We did not carry socks, underwear, pajamas, etc. In 1947, we added custom-made blouses for women. Three years later, one of our man-tailored blouses appeared on the cover of *Life*—it was the feature story.

## ON NEGOTIATING A DEAL

The fact that I now own eighty-one stores coast-to-coast, with no partners, no stockholders, no franchises, and no competitors, indicates that my start-up problems obviously were resolved, and for this I have to thank Andrew Seligson, at least in part.

A deal must have advantages for each of the two parties involved. If it turns out to be one-sided, then the "injured" party sulks, rebels, loses motivation, or just drops out. The injury festers and the deal no longer works. It really is a mistake to be greedy. Seligson was greedy and lost a chance to buy half of The Custom Shop for $10,000. It would have earned him $50 million. I turned down his offer because it wasn't equitable; it wasn't a fair deal. He was arrogant and, as it turned out, stupid. I saved $50 million and continued my personal ego trip as founder and sole owner.

I had been in business for two months. My head was bloodied but unbowed, when in walked an apparition. He was wearing a bowler hat, a black Chesterfield coat with a velvet collar, a starched white shirt collar, a handsome black tie with small white polka dots, yellow chamois gloves, and a furled umbrella. He was about thirty-five, short, dapper, and looked like he could take on the world. He asked, "Are you the proprietor?"

"Yes," I replied.

"It's an interesting idea you have here. My name is Andrew Seligson; I was in charge of the custom shirt department at Saks Fifth Avenue, and am presently in charge of the custom shirt department at Freems of the Waldorf. [At the time, one of New York's most expensive clothing stores, located at the Waldorf-Astoria on Park Avenue.] If you would like a partner, I'd be interested, and I know everything there is to know about the custom shirt business."

I said, "Unfortunately, I know practically nothing about the custom shirt business, but I really don't want a partner."

"Perhaps we can work something out."

"Perhaps we can. I intend to open thirty-five stores. We can form a partnership, but only for store number two—no part of store number one or my workrooms."

Seligson said, "That would be okay. Let me work with you for the next two months. I'll work for nothing—let's say twenty-five dollars a week—and if this is as good as it looks, we'll draw up a contract."

"Great."

So Seligson came in. Although I had been learning fast, it's fair to say that Seligson took over immediately. At the end of two months, he brought in his accountant. Together they told me I was bankrupt. Seligson said my business needed $10,000 in additional capital. His proposal: He would put up $5,000; I would put up $5,000, and we would then be fifty-fifty partners in the *entire* business, including my factory and my present store.

I said to him: "But, Andrew, that wouldn't be at all equitable. You must put up five thousand dollars, but only for a half-interest in the *second* store. It's my idea, and it's my business, and I am *not* bankrupt."

Seligson replied: "Mortimer, your idea is great, but you haven't the foggiest idea of what you're doing. You can't possibly continue without my expertise, or without additional capital. If you don't agree, I'll open up in competition; you'll never survive."

My father-in-law said, "Mortimer, you are not a businessman. I'll lend you the five thousand dollars. Take Seligson in." I was almost in tears. "*It's not equitable,*" I said, "and I can't do it. I don't need the five thousand dollars, but thanks anyway." Seligson walked out, opining, "You'll rue the day."

Seligson's accountant had calculated that the customer's deposits were a *liability*, since it was money I owed until I delivered the shirts. From an accounting point of view, he was right; but as a pragmatic neophyte, I knew he was wrong, because all those sales would be concluded, and profitably—and they were. I borrowed no money from my father-in-law, nor anyone else—not then, not ever—and three and a half years later opened my ninth store. It was in Philadelphia. There I inadvertently learned that Seligson was managing a small ladies' hosiery shop on Chestnut Street. I never again heard from him. Of such decisions are men's lives and fortunes made. Think about it—what a chance he passed up. The truth is, he looked bright, but he wasn't; he had squeezed too hard, to a point of diminishing return. He knew more about shirtmaking, but he lacked the heart of an entrepreneur.

Considering my ridiculously shaky start, it might be reasonable to think that Somebody was in my corner. Yet I would not want you to conclude that my subsequent success was due to heavenly intervention, or even luck, although it is obvious that I was marginally financed (when I conceived the idea, I *did* have $10,000) and not really prepared to start The Custom Shop. Yet, as it turned out, I have contributed many innovative concepts that were totally new to the way things had been done by other shirtmakers. And they are responsible for sustaining Custom Shop's unique success.

Almost forty years later, in 1976, I realized that quite a few men had stopped wearing neckties in New York City on weekends, even in some of the better restaurants. I remember the very first time I saw a man walking on Fifth Avenue in Bermuda shorts, I was shocked. In my day, T-shirts were worn only as undershirts. Suddenly, they were replacing sport shirts. Massive changes were taking place —men in advertising were wearing jeans to the office. Should the time come to pass that men stopped wearing neckties at the office, there would be small need for custom-made shirts. So in 1977 I took a defensive step by expanding our line to offer customers custom-made suits. This move picked up our volume by 25 percent.

Of course, I had to answer the old question of why customers should come to me for their custom-made suits instead of where they had been going. The answer was relatively easy:

1. I can make custom-made suits for less than other custom tailors. *All* custom tailors buy their fabrics at retail. That is, they buy their woolens from a jobber, because they don't use sufficient quantity to buy directly from the mill. Because I have so many stores, we use sufficient quantity to buy directly from the mill, the same mill from which the jobbers buy. As there are three and a half to four yards in a suit, we can save the customer $100 to $150, depending on the quality he chooses.
2. The customer coming to us for a custom-made shirt comes because he usually has a fit problem, and he is, therefore, a natural for custom-made suits. When we measure him for shirts, we have him with his jacket

off. It is convenient for him to slip on a jacket that can point up or correct his fit problems.

3. Because a color coordination service is an important part of our business, we are in position to color-coordinate suit, shirt, and tie, a very important plus, because the customer will always look better if his clothes are color-coordinated. They seldom are, because the subject has never been part of the college curriculum.

At this point in The Custom Shop's life, about 80 percent of our branches carry our custom-made suits. It is a decision I am happy to have made.

There are some other reasons why I believe The Custom Shop continues to be a success. Our prices are actually 30 to 50 percent less than the other shirtmakers. They mostly buy from a contractor who obviously must make a profit. In contrast, I sell to my own stores at no profit. Yet, surprisingly, high-priced upstairs shirtmakers (currently offering custom-made shirts at $125 to $200) have more complaints about fit than we do. They get back about eighteen shirts out of a hundred; we get back about six—5.64, to be exact.

Perhaps I had better explain. To begin with, the tape measure is misleading. It can take the body's measurements, but it *cannot* measure the body's *configuration*. Therefore, upstairs shirtmakers make a sample shirt first. The customer tries on the sample shirt, then the shirtmaker changes the pattern in accordance with the customer's wishes. Presumably, the customer will then have a perfect shirt. In practice, that does not happen.

For example, Barbara Gelb wrote this remarkable account of her husband's joy and his ensuing frustration when he ordered custom-made shirts from Turnbull & Asser, London's most prestigious shirtmaker. The article (reprinted here in part) appeared in the *New York Times* in January 1985:

Yet, however carefully you are measured by Mr. Curr, or by Robert Squires, one of his assistants, there are *always* little adjustments to be made in the finished product. Indeed, it will very likely be *six months* before the *sample* shirt is pronounced wearable.

My husband's *first* shirt was mailed to him in New York about *two months* after he was measured. He unfolded it reverently. It was a deep, glowing pink with tiny white checks. [*We carry the identical fabrics.*] The cotton was smooth and supple, the cut generously full [*most men who order shirts custom-made do not want it cut "generously full"; they want it perfectly fitted in the chest and waist*], the stitching sturdy and almost invisible. [*No one sees the stitching because it is always invisible and always sturdy.*] When he slipped it on he instinctively stood taller.

The fit, however, was not perfect. What was acceptable in an $18 shirt became impermissible in one costing over $75 [*Turnbull & Asser's shirts are now $90 ready-made, $125 to $200 custom-made*]. The collar was a bit high in back; the points were a trifle too long; the cuffs buttoned a mite too snugly.

He dictated some imperious notes to me regarding these minor deficiencies, and I, agreeing that we should not overlook the most trifling flaw (nor would Turnbull & Asser wish us to), then mailed back the shirt with written instructions for adjustment. The shirt was returned several weeks later. This time the cuffs buttoned a bit *too* loosely and the collar was a smidgen *too tight*. Once again, I sent the shirt back with instructions. (Italics mine.)

This kind of back-and-forth mailing is evidently routine. "Our shirts know their way across the Atlantic," wrote Mr. Williams. The beautiful pink shirt was returned again after several months, with a courteous letter suggesting that my husband wear it, have it laundered, and *then* judge the fit.

The average shirtmaker will ask, for example, "How do you like your shirts to fit—snug or easy?" Well, neither "easy" nor "snug" is a measurement. We give the customer a fitting *before* we make the shirt. He can *demonstrate* the fit he prefers on the shell we give him to put on. Then we do the same thing with collars. Unlike other shirtmakers, we give our customers an assortment of various collars to try on. That way it becomes easy to determine the most flattering back height, front height, collar size, and finally, collar style. Like a Polaroid camera, the customer sees the results at once. Actually, he sees it *before* we make it.

## EARLY COMPETITION

There have been more than twenty-five individuals and/or companies who have tried to compete directly with The Custom Shop. Even the major-leaguers failed. Let's take a look at the three billion-dollar conglomerates that tried.

International Industries (the House of Pancakes, the House of Nines, et al.) was approached by Jim Auerbach, at that time manager of my Beverly Hills store, with the idea of setting up a competitive chain. Jim knew my system thoroughly, and Bill Cavanaugh, my plant manager who joined Jim, knew exactly how we made our shirts.

So Jim and Bill, with International Industries putting up the money, opened up thirty-one stores called The Shirt Gallery. They didn't actually open thirty branches; rather, they sold franchises to misguided entrepreneurs. Half the branches were company-owned. The Shirt Gallery failed for several reasons:

1. Wherever they opened a branch, a Custom Shop already existed, which means they had to live off my dissatisfied customers (certainly not more than 10 percent). And if there was no Custom Shop there, it usually meant that we had already dismissed the location as marginal.
2. Their prices were higher than mine because their costs were higher. Because the stores were franchised, their factory had to make a profit selling to the franchisee.
3. Their people were never properly trained: they had only two weeks of training. My people go to school for five months before they are permitted to take measurements on their own.
4. The Shirt Gallery was the "new kid on the block." The Custom Shop had already been around for twenty years.
5. No one in their organization had any taste. Therefore, there was no comparison between the image projected by their stores and The Custom Shop. In addition to a lack of taste, they lacked capital. They spent $75,000 to open a store; we spent $150,000.

After four years, The Shirt Gallery folded—bankrupt.

The second billion-dollar conglomerate was Genesco. Walton Maxey Jarman, the chairman, made the mistake of moving from a very profitable wholesale shoe-manufacturing empire into retailing. Against my advice, he bought a great many men's clothing stores (Rogers Kent, Whitehouse & Hardy, Frank Brothers, et al., most of them now out of business) and two clothing manufacturers. My first Custom Shop executive vice president, George Zimmerman, suggested to Maxey that he open a factory like Custom Shop's and offer custom-made shirts in all his clothing stores. He did, but that was not profitable either, because Maxey's factory also had to make a profit, meaning that his prices were 30 percent higher than mine for the identical product.

Like The Shirt Gallery, Maxey asked me to buy his factory and his business, and once again I said no. Genesco gave up after seven years, selling that division to Spencer Hayes, a successful Bible salesman from the West.

Conglomerate number three, W. R. Grace, bought an old-line, marginal, custom shirtmaker named Packard Shirts, located in Kansas City. Packard's custom-made shirts were sold by independent salesmen who called on businessmen at their offices. W. R. Grace tried to update that marginal business by adding mail-order. They lost about $6 million and gave up after four years of trying a variety of different approaches. They wanted to sell me their factory and their inventory. I had no interest, and they just closed up.

I opened up my own competition long before any of the others. In 1947, I bought a new men's shop called deFrees, a much more elegant store than any of The Custom Shops I had at that time. DeFrees had a corner location (I'd never had one) on Madison Avenue at Fifty-sixth Street. DeFrees had been opened originally by Irwin Friedlander, Custom Shop's second executive vice president. I bought him out, and brought him back to run The Custom Shop. We installed custom-made shirts in deFrees (Friedlander carried only ready-mades; he was too smart to try and compete by using a contractor), and charged fifty cents more than we charged at The Custom Shop. We had a successful first year. I then watched the custom shirt business go down in 1948 and down again in 1949. In 1950, I changed the name to The Custom Shop: same location. Sales shot up immediately. I knew way back then that I would probably never have a successful competitor. The Custom Shop had arrived.

Ever since 1941, the year I switched from chief operating officer to chief executive officer, I have received letters and phone calls from companies and individuals interested in buying The Custom Shop. I had no interest in selling then, nor will I sell any part of the business while I am alive. When I die, my estate will put The Custom Shop on the market, but I have left instructions to favor Custom Shop's president, Anthony Bergamo, with whom I have worked for almost ten years.

Happily, Tony turned out to be a soul mate, even though we are quite different. Tony's equivalent of my interest in tennis, skiing, music, writing, sailing, and fashion is wrapped up in one *intense* interest: business! And that business happens to be The Custom Shop. Obviously, it's an interest that we share equally. The difference is that he has the ability—no, the desire—to give it his all by working at it. I give it my all by standing apart, looking at it carefully, watching it, searching out its weaknesses, and then coming up with suggestions to make it better. It has happened time and time again that I have said, "This is it; this is the ultimate. Now it really is fixed"—whatever—only to find that it wasn't, at which point I would come up with another fix.

A good idea deserves constant watching, and an entrepreneur's inner drive will always keep trying to make it better and better.

# 4

. □ .

# Lessons in Failure

I've described my success and offered some reasons for it. Let's see if there is anything to be learned by looking at some of my failures. They were not fatal to the business, fortunately, but they did hurt.

## FAILURES IN ADVERTISING

Should you advertise? My experience says no. My national business grew only by word of mouth, because we did *no* advertising at all out of town. And in New York, only a small (two columns by three inches) twice-monthly ad in the *New York Times*. I tried it (on and off, mostly off) from 1947 to 1971. We stopped advertising altogether in 1972, and our business actually shot up—not exactly another case of cause and effect, although that's what it seemed to have been at the time.

Yet The Custom Shop would seem to be the perfect business to advertise, as we actually have a product worth advertising, with a service and a price that no one else can match. "Custom-made" projects an image of chauffeur-driven limousines, but The Custom Shop's low prices have clearly brought "custom-made" into the reach of the workaday world.

New customers who respond to an ad because of the headline or copy must then look for the address. My addresses were always set in the smallest possible type size, at the very bottom of each ad. I had twelve Manhattan locations in 1947, and at the end of the twelve addresses, the customer would find this:

Advertising test for new customers only. Bring this ad for a 10% discount. Offer expires in two weeks.

I divided the number of responses into the cost of the ad and came up with a most disappointing figure. The cost of bringing in one new customer from my *New York Times* ad was $84; average sale was $200; pretax profit $20. Obviously, my advertising was a losing proposition. The same advertising tests done in Chicago and Los Angeles turned out to be even worse.

In any case, one day early in 1985, while making out a contribution to one of my favorite art organizations, I thought, Why not give away some money to myself? Why not advertise again, even if it doesn't pay, just for the pleasure of seeing The Custom Shop name in the papers? So I worked up a whole new series of ads, and this time tested those ads in thirty cities. And as had happened in the distant past, the results were dismal. I tried, all told, eight different approaches, and the results were pretty much the same.

A *New York Times* ad covered not only New York City but the entire metropolitan area, the surrounding suburbs, plus Baltimore, Washington, Atlanta, Miami, Fort Lauderdale, Boston, Hartford, Stamford, Hackensack, Short Hills, and Philadelphia. Despite all that hoopla, the best result I could manage in 1986 was an average cost of $84 per customer. Once again, I was spending $84 to earn a $20 profit.

How could it be that the whole world advertised, most of it *pretending* a competitive advantage that did not truly exist? If they found it profitable to advertise, why didn't I, who really did have a competitive edge? I have yet to speak with an advertising man who could give me a sensible answer to that question. I have opened fifty stores out of town without a single opening ad or even a piece of direct mail to announce the opening.

## DIRECT-MAIL TURNABOUT

Twice a year, we sent our customers a twelve-page brochure-style catalogue so they could reorder by mail: full color, on heavy glossy stock—quite handsome. We mailed out about 200,000 pieces each time. In 1984, the cost was about $80,000, but the return was only $100,000, and that percentage return had been about the same for the past twenty years. Obviously, my direct-mail advertising was not paying for itself either. I don't know why I continued it for so long.

Nor do I understand why it wasn't successful. For the most part, men do not like to shop, and we were making it so easy for them. We had their measurements. The color reproduction of our best-selling shirtings was excellent, and there was a choice of different collar styles and shirts that would really fit. Our business would seem to be a *natural* for direct mail. Yet it never worked. After having been in business fifty years, I finally found an answer. Not an answer as to why the customers did not order by mail, but a way to increase their response by 700 percent.

Instead of sending out a twelve-page folder that included not only our custom shirt fabrics, but also neckties, blouses, and ready-made shirts—I eliminated everything except our custom shirtings and reduced the production costs from $80,000 to $40,000. I used the $40,000 I saved to offer a 10 percent discount, but *only* to customers who reordered by *mail*. I passed on the savings that were effected in by-passing store overhead.

Who would believe that a "miserly" 10 percent discount (at a time when newspaper ads and television commercials were regularly offering discounts of 40, 50, and even 60 percent), would be so effective? Would you have thought that 10 percent could be so meaningful? Immediately, my mail-order sales jumped from $100,000 to $700,000. Of course, that made us all feel very good, but why had it taken me so long? Perhaps because we have never run a sale on anything custom-made, and, in effect, this seemed like a sale. Actually, the customer had to forgo the personal service of a designer consultation. And for many of them, it was a mistake because a personal visit would have "updated" the fit to compensate for any changes in weight and permit some further experimenting in collar styling.

## FAILURES IN COMMUNICATION

I made two errors early on. They were not fatal, but mistakes I never should have made. The first was the name I decided on—The Custom Shop. In retrospect, the name was a mistake for two reasons:

First, "The Custom Shop" is completely impersonal, unlike, for example, "David London, Shirtmaker." Even "Mortimer Levitt, Shirtmaker" would have been better, although (not wanting to be a businessman) I would never have used my own name. If people remember the name at all, they think of us incorrectly as "The Custom Shirt Shop." The name (The Custom Shop) also has the unfortunate overtones of "English Tea Shoppe"—not very prestigious. Happily, everyone seems to know my trademark, the little striped-dome awning.

My second mistake was that very first window ad of which I had been so proud. "We have devised a method whereby we can afford . . ." That simple phrase, "devised a method," gave other shirtmakers and haberdashers free rein to speculate on what that method might be. And they came up with an endless series of pot shots, preposterous stories about how we could do it for so little money. The myth is still so ingrained that even our own completely satisfied customers sometimes say, "Well, of course, your shirts are not *really* custom-made." And to this day, that problem has never been resolved, even though, at my request, the *New York Times*, the Better Business Bureau, and the Federal Trade Commission sent investigators to my workrooms where they saw, with their own eyes, that every shirt was individually cut to the thirteen individual measurements taken by our designers. As a result, complaints that had been filed with the Better Business Bureau and the Federal Trade Commission were withdrawn, and the *Times* continued to accept our ads stating that Custom Shop shirts were indeed custom-made.

## FAILURES IN RECRUITING TOP MANAGEMENT

Since I retired in 1941 as chief operating officer, there have been five men who functioned in that post. From 1941 to

1959, I made the mistake of trusting the business to three men who, because of their lack of experience as merchandisers, were not effective. Then in 1959, I hired Glenn Bernbaum. He was a pro, my first, and he ran the company until 1979, when he was replaced by Anthony Bergamo, Custom Shop's current president. I am ashamed to write this, but if Bergamo were knocked out of the box tomorrow, I would once again have to recruit my chief operating officer from outside. The business would continue to run, of course, on its own momentum, with the staff doing the routine things it had been doing all along. But a business must keep up with changing times, and that demands a chief executive with an eye to see, an ear to hear, a brain to simplify the chaos, and the ability to resolve the endless series of problems that every business confronts.

I have complained to friends and other entrepreneurs about my inability to find an understudy for my president, and without exception, their response has been, "Well, that's Bergamo's mistake," as if to say the power and responsibility are overly centralized at The Custom Shop. That answer is a cliché. It took me eighteen years to find Glenn Bernbaum, and then three years to find Anthony Bergamo after I decided that Glenn had to resign because Mortimer's, his restaurant, demanded full attention. There is no person more aware of the need for a second-in-command than Tony. He finds himself working literally seven days and seven nights a week. Recently, I insisted that he take a place in the country to use as a weekend retreat. So he bought a house in New Jersey—close to our factory.

So far, we have been unable to find a person with that extra something needed in a chief operating officer, a person who possesses both the image and the substance of a leader. Without such a person, the business is not in safe hands and its future is precarious.

Unfortunately, my personnel problems don't end with the

chief operating officer or the chief executive officer. I also need about twelve new managers and twelve assistant managers every year. We have eighty-one stores, with new stores opening regularly. We project that 10 percent of our managers and assistant managers will resign or be asked to resign every year—a normal turnover. Experience tells us that we must hire seventy-two to replace the twenty-four. And then, of course, of those twenty-four who do become managers or assistant managers, only six will last five years. That's because our key people are frequently lured away by our customers, businessmen who are astonished to find "sales clerks" with such a high degree of competence (a direct result of our excellent training program).

Partly because of this continuing turnover, I have not been successful in creating in my own stores the ambience, that feeling of family, the friendliness and warmth one finds in the Ed Mitchell store in Westport, Connecticut (where we spend the summers), or the original Neiman-Marcus store in Dallas. In both cases, the owners were there in person. Despite all the effort we put into training, management cannot be in all our stores in person, and we have yet to find a substitute that is as effective as having the proprietor on the premises.

My key people are sought after because they have been so well trained. It was very hard to replace those plant managers who left us to join up with the many competitors who opened imitation Custom Shops. They would offer my people a 50 percent salary increase—sometimes more. And we can't hire experienced teachers or experienced plant managers, because there is no other business quite like mine. So it is always a real shock to lose one of our key people, even a good manager.

At least a dozen of those managers took our customers' files. They knew those measurements would be helpful if they went into business for themselves, calling on customers at their offices. Actually, there is no one I know of who has yet made that approach pay off long term.

There is one additional factor that tends to make a cooperative spirit difficult, if not impossible, in companies that have been unionized, as mine has. Union members pay dues, and there comes a time when the membership begins to resent paying dues. To prevent that, unions must attempt to make employers out to be villains. No matter how generous an employer might want to be, the union finds a way to justify its own existence by making the employer out to be an adversary.

McDonald's comes closest to an efficient handling of its personnel problem. McDonald's by-passes personality by basing service on the efficiency of its assembly-line approach. There is also a chain in the Northeast called the Friendly stores that seems to maintain a family spirit. They offer forty flavors of ice cream, light food—sandwiches, salads, lunch and dinner specialties, etc. Friendly restaurants are staffed mostly by college students during summers and holidays, and college graduates who fill in while looking for regular employment. "Friendly is the name, and Friendly is the game." They have been quite successful in establishing a certain camaraderie to which the new help immediately responds.

## THE FAILURE TO COMMUNICATE "MY MESSAGE" TO CUSTOMERS AFTER FIFTY YEARS OF TRYING

Although my business has been enormously successful, and obviously I have made and continue to make pots of money, more than the compensation received by the chief executive officer at General Motors, Du Pont, you name it, there are *two* aspects of my business that have been endlessly frustrating.

First, we make our customer a shirt that is perfectly fitted with a collar that has been individually designed to make him look his best. Then the customer *usually undoes everything we have tried to do for him.* He *ruins* the shirt because: (1) He uses the cheapest possible laundry, or no laundry at all (his wife). Frequently, the collar is almost mutilated —not maliciously, but mutilated nevertheless. (2) He doesn't *know* how to color-coordinate his shirt, tie, and suit. Yet he rejects our effort to educate him. He thinks we want to teach him The Custom Shop Knot only to sell him neckties. He rejects our advice too because he has been traumatized, originally by his mother ("John, you come back here this instant and change your clothes; you may *not* go out looking like that," etc.). Subsequently, he gets more of the same from his wife. Every Saturday, in every Custom Shop throughout the land, disgruntled wives drag husbands in by the ear, saying, "Do *something*. I can't bear to look at him another minute."

My second frustration has to do with our reorders. Considering our low price, and our minuscule percentage of adjustments, we should expect a 85 percent reorder rate. Yet it averages less, and I *know* we deserve better. There are two probable reasons: (1) As I have already said, customers do not wear our shirts to their best advantage. (2) Our designers are frequently too busy to establish the kind of personal relationship with the customer that they should. As shirtmakers and designers, we are professionals in the same sense that an architect or interior decorator is a professional. We are actually "exterior" decorators. But customers have been conditioned to think of us as salesmen, because they automatically think of men in a men's store as salesmen.

My advice for new customers would be that they insist on having measurements taken by the manager, not necessarily because he is better, but because he will have had more experience than the assistant manager.

## MY BIGGEST AND MOST
## DISAPPOINTING FAILURE

I have been conducting seminars for many years at Fortune 500 companies and at major universities on the subject of image. I am usually greeted with more hostility than curiosity. The same men who pay for the advice of architects, advertising agencies, etc., take the advice we offer as *personal* criticism, the kind they have had too much of from Mom and "the wife."

Yet my seminars did lead to a super idea. If it had been successful, it would have done more to turn The Custom Shop into an international institution than anything that had gone before. And I am still devastated because, after trying so hard for almost ten years, I've concluded that it just can't be done.

The concept was simple.

I know (and believe me, I know it only too well, because I have been looking at the images projected by executives for some fifty years) that the image projected by executives seldom does justice to their status.

An M.B.A. spends eighteen years at school to earn that prestigious title. And his six years of college cost about $200,000 in pretax dollars (add up the loss of earning power during those six years to the cost of tuition, room and board). Eighteen years of education for an M.B.A. degree, but not a single hour was spent on how to *look* like an M.B.A.

Men look their *very* best in uniforms: military, judicial, clerical, and, of course, evening clothes, black tie or white tie, all of which make man look his best, because they all by-pass a man's personal taste. More specifically, they by-pass his lack of education in dressing himself. Yet executives could look just as impressive in their business uniforms if they understood my few simple concepts.

The need is there. We see it every day at The Custom Shop, and I see it twice a week at our home when our overachieving friends come to dinner.

I learned very quickly that even though my seminar is interesting and instructive, a man cannot learn to dress himself by attending such a seminar, any more than he can learn to hit a golf ball by spending an hour with a pro who says, in effect, "Now here is how you do it," and proceeds to hit the ball 275 yards.

So I came up with a plan by which the company would pay for a two-and-a-half-hour individual-image consultation for any executive who wanted it. A completely color-coordinated wardrobe plan for summer, winter, spring, and fall, for business, weekends, and all social occasions. In addition, the executive would also get a *one-time only* 20 percent discount on custom-made suits, custom-made shirts and neckties, merchandise that is *never, ever* on sale. The fee to the corporation would be $100. The executive would be saving $200 on a $1,000 order, which would undoubtedly be an average purchase, at least for the man ordering suits and shirts and ties.

Now what is the advantage of all this to The Custom Shop? We don't *need* that business, and in the case of the $1,000 order, we would actually be losing $100. However —and this is the point—we would be developing a whole group of overachievers who really did *look* like overachievers. These are the opinion leaders, leaders who have now seen the light, men who are no longer insecure about dressing themselves, men who could now shop without their wives. These are the men who would make Custom Shop famous, executives who would become our personal missionaries by spreading Custom Shop's gospel. It is a great idea, and it was a complete and total failure, because most executives have been traumatized by their mothers in the beginning, and their wives later on. Result: the whole subject of "dressing" is anathema, and they run away from it.

For all the fifty years that The Custom Shop has been in business, people have been under the impression that we are in the shirt business. Not so. Mainly, we are in the image business, a *service* business. If we don't improve the image of our customer, he goes elsewhere.

The problems involved in running a business have been, and will continue to be, endless. Resolving problems as they occur is the price one pays for being the proprietor, the price you pay for owning your own business. But the rewards are well worth the effort. I think you'll discover this as we examine the experiences of sixteen highly successful entrepreneurs in the pages that follow. And I expect, too, that you will enjoy the diversity—the wide variety of examples I have chosen.

ARTHUR IMPERATORE, *chairman of the board, A-P-A Transport*

# 5

■ □ ■

# ARTHUR IMPERATORE
## Obsessive Drive Converts
## an Army Truck into a
## Transportation Empire

Arthur Imperatore projects a quiet, laid-back, rather sleepy image, totally at odds with the ambitious, aggressive man within. He does not follow my formula for success, because he really had no exciting reason for opening his own trucking business: he had no angle. Yet his obsessive behavior, his relentless drive to make his business a success is an important lesson to would-be entrepreneurs. Without this all-consuming drive, few new business ideas, even brilliant ones, would get off the ground.

Imperatore began as one of seven children born to first-generation Italian immigrants. His father scratched out a living as a baker in West New York, New Jersey. A $2 million yacht, called the *Imperator*, is an indication of his status at the age of sixty. His firm, A-P-A Transport Company, is the third most profitable trucking company in the country. Arthur enjoys his success without inhibition. He has his own chauffeur-driven Rolls-Royce, and an opulent office done in seventeenth-century Venetian style. In addition to all this, he also owns 366 acres of waterfront property on the Hudson River directly across from midtown Manhattan and is currently in the process of developing this fabulous tract. The project is expected to take decades to complete and carries a $5 billion price tag. Quite an accomplishment considering Imperatore's modest beginnings. It would be nice to say, "That's America," but chances are that Arthur would have made it wherever he had been born. Anyway, here's how "going into business" happened to Arthur.

In 1946, when he returned from his World War II soldiering, Imperatore found that two of his older brothers owned an Army surplus truck, a truck that they had picked up for a song. And soon after that, his two remaining brothers also bought an Army surplus truck. The four of them joined forces as Imperatore Brothers Trucking. They had a modest stipend from the government as a result of their honorable discharges: $20 a week for each of them for one year following their return to civilian life.

Arthur worked as a full-time Fuller Brush salesman by day, while majoring in three subjects at night in City College. He was working hard, perhaps too hard, at both his job and his school, which is probably the reason he overreacted one day when he came home to find his brothers "hanging out" in the kitchen. "They were not out beating the bushes to get business," he recalls. "I was furious and told them so in no uncertain terms. I told them, 'Get my name off those trucks or get out there and work!' " The brothers had always looked up to Arthur, even though he was next to the youngest, because Arthur was driven—he was obsessed. Still, it is hard to believe this twenty-one-year-old would become the motivating force that built one of the most profitable trucking empires in the entire country. (A-P-A's after-tax profits are a remarkable 10 percent, 300 percent higher than the industry average.)

Arthur always wanted desperately to make money. He actually opened his first bank account when he was ten years old with money earned by running errands, or whatever odd jobs he could find. According to his sister Anna Kortrey, "While other children played, Arthur was saying 'I want to be a millionaire' and was willing to work hard if that's what it took to make money."

The questions you might want to ask yourself are, Do I have this kind of ambition? Do I want my own business that badly? I know that I didn't, not really. I knew only that I was *not* destined to live and die in Brooklyn, but it was all talk, daydreams. I was nothing, really. It was only after I started The Custom Shop that I discovered certain abilities that, until then, I had not been aware of. Nor did I foresee that I would become a retired multimillionaire at the age of thirty-four and then be so unhappy I would spend two years with a psychoanalyst. People have different needs, different aptitudes, and different motivations. Some people make it the easy way. Others, like Arthur Imperatore, make it the hard way.

The early days of their business were rough. The brothers grabbed work wherever they could find it, mostly short hauls of household goods, but they were not doing very well. The trucking industry was already jam-packed with competition, other veterans having similarly bought up Army surplus trucks. It was at this point that Imperatore decided to drop out of school and join the company full-time. He threw his savings into the pot and appointed himself president of the new company. He laid down his first rule—"The people with the most merit get the most say"—and announced that since he was the smartest one in the family, he was taking over the business. Incredible! Arthur decided they would be better off by specializing in one form of transport: moving freight. He decided to buy the A & P Trucking Corporation for $800. Arthur realized that the new name, A & P Trucking, would give them a chance to capitalize on the instant recognition of the much advertised A & P supermarket chain. That $800 acquisition also included several beat-up trucks along with four much-needed loading docks.

Competition was fierce. A slogan frequently painted on the sides of trucks in those days, CRIME DOESNT PAY AND NEITHER DOES TRUCKING, may give you some small idea of the marginal business the brothers were in. The only way to get business was by hustling, "and once I took over," Arthur said, "we all worked like animals."

It was Arthur who went out knocking on the doors of manufacturers who might be making daily shipments. He was looking for a more stable source of work. He solicited by phone too: "I've got trucks; we're moving goods. We can do it better, and it will cost you less." Imperatore was relentless in his search for freight. He landed a bottling company, a battery company, and a painting firm.

With his hard-sell, won't-take-no-for-an-answer approach, the business grew. As the fleet expanded, so did their docking needs. Much of the maintenance work on the antiquated trucks had been performed on streets by lantern light. Then happenstance came into play. The postwar economy moved into high gear, much to the advantage of their business.

By 1949, A & P had outgrown its modest loading docks, and they erected a terminal in North Bergen. And when the opportunity came along, they also bought out three tiny truckers in New England.

Thanks to the surge in business, Arthur and his brothers were working eighteen-hour days. They were constantly understaffed, partly due, of course, to Arthur's exacting standards. Scenes with an enraged Arthur (similar to the one that had occurred in the Imperatore kitchen) were replayed again and again. But now the audience was not only older brothers, it also included many employees.

The trucking industry had a relatively recent network of interstate highways: a new territory to be charted. A-P-A Trucking (the name change was forced in 1955 after a costly legal battle, but the firm had the use of the name A & P for some seven years), along with other trucking firms, worked their drivers to the bone. The industry became ripe for unionization.

Imperatore had not yet acquired his respect for humankind and was determined to resist unionization. He was an outspoken adversary of "make-work" and "gold-bricking." He threatened his workers with loss of their jobs if they struck. They struck anyway, and he learned a lesson: Never give an ultimatum that you cannot or do not intend to carry out. Arthur now concedes that he was a demanding employer, perhaps too demanding. He bowed to unionization. At the same time, the union gained respect for him, because he stood up for his views with courage and integrity.

There was a particular reason for Imperatore's unique success—that is, his high profit margin. It was his commitment to making a science out of the delivery of freight, along with his relentless energy. He used time and motion studies to analyze every movement necessary to move a package from the moment of taking an order to the arrival at its destination. It's hard to believe, but he found there were 224 separate movements. He established an optimal performance level, after which he then instituted a daily system of industrial-engineering checks to see that each worker produced at optimal level. Each worker had to give almost 100 percent for the system to be effective. Today these standards are met or even exceeded by 96 percent of A-P-A's workers.

Finally, and most important, Imperatore computerized

his monitoring system. The system receives information from tracking devices that tell management the amount of time a truck is moving, the amount of time the truck is stopped, cruising speeds, rpm, etc. Arthur would return the individual record to a worker who was not producing, "because the figures don't lie." Loiterers, cheats, and liars are not tolerated. If there is a legitimate excuse, it's accepted —once. Twice, and the worker may face dismissal. Interestingly enough, once the early days of unionization passed, Arthur never had another problem with the union. His practices were deemed to be fair because they were based on objective criteria.

I believe that lengthy interviews of prospective employees are a waste of executive time and company money. Neither the employee nor the employer knows in advance what the employee's performance will be like until he or she is actually on the job. Then too I lost any respect I may have had for "psychological testing." In 1946, The Custom Shop engaged the services of a company specializing in psychological testing. They would evaluate the new applicants we were ready to hire. Then we discovered that two of the employees who received the testing company's approval were mistakes: one was an alcoholic and the other a recent inmate of a mental institution. I discontinued all such testing for good.

Imperatore, however, believes that personnel problems can be most easily solved by very careful screening, and the interview process at A-P-A eliminates all but the "cleanest" of applicants. His approach was appropriate for an industry that tended to attract some pretty tough men. Imperatore wanted "no bad apples working for me." Even today, only 4 percent of all applicants are considered viable candidates for A-P-A, and only half of those make it to the company as probationary employees. Polygraph tests are given, and urinalysis tests are performed to weed out drug users. The applicant's name is checked against a computerized list of more than 1 million arrest records—sifted from crime news columns in thirty-five newspapers. Personal references are also checked against that list. Any applicant unfortunate enough to list an untoward reference is usually rejected. Word is out about the list, however, and would-be workers who associate with criminals don't apply, or are smart enough not to list criminals as personal references.

Today Arthur Imperatore owns more than 90 percent of the stock in A-P-A Transport. His fortune is estimated at $200 million. He was lucky to find the proper outlet for all that bottled-up energy. In addition to energy, Arthur had other qualities:

1. An aptitude for organizing and especially for simplifying.
2. An ability to be tough if toughness is called for.
3. An aptitude for evaluating people accurately.
4. Insomnia, giving him more hours to work in a day.
5. An ability to motivate, partially by example, but to a great extent by reinforcement of exceptional performance.
6. A genuine interest in his employees, which manifests itself in exceptional employee benefits, including a fully equipped, super-deluxe gymnasium, as well as expense-paid cruises for employees and spouses.
7. An eye to the future, not only for innovations within the trucking industry, but also for the U.S. economy.

For most entrepreneurs, the story of A-P-A would be the beginning—and the end. But Imperatore is also a visionary, a fact that emerged when in 1981 he started buying real estate. Under the name Arcorp Properties, he bought the

366-acre tract which he calls the "tail of New Jersey." The strip of land is on the Hudson on the Weehawken/West New York waterfront, paralleling the waterfront from Thirty-eighth Street to Seventy-fourth Street in Manhattan. Right now, it is filled with dozens of warehouses and terminals, a potter's field for the industries that had at one time dominated the Hudson Valley.

Setting a thirty-year goal, Imperatore plans to build a city with a European flavor. It would consist of 15,000 apartment units, 10 million square feet of office space, and a new ferryboat service (it began service in 1986 despite opposition from New York City developers) between New Jersey and Manhattan. To help him create his master plan, Imperatore brought in four prestigious experts: Cesar Pelli, recently retired dean of Yale's School of Architecture; J. Robert Hillier, an architect from Princeton; Rodney Friedman, a waterfront designer; and Jonathan Barnett, an urban designer.

Will Arthur be able to pull this awesome project together? I suspect the answer will be a big "And how!" And he relishes the challenge. "It's as if I've spent a whole lifetime, at least a business lifetime," he says, "getting ready to do something important."

A true entrepreneur is seldom satisfied. At first, his objective might be money; but he doesn't usually stop there —even though he has accumulated more than he will ever need. Does Imperatore, who really loves his trucking business, *need* to move into a project of such enormous proportions, faced with endless problems, endless decisions, and undoubtedly considerable risk? You can answer that question better after you too have made it on your own.

# 6

■ □ ■

# JOSEPH KOHLER
## A "Burma Shave" Advertising Twist Worth $2.5 Million

Joseph Kohler III took a half-baked idea that came to him by happenstance and baked it properly. Seeing the potential for using the towers that support chair lifts at ski areas as billboards, he introduced soft-sell advertising to the slopes and made millions.

Joe is an example of a young man who, while working dutifully for others, took a chance on moving out when an opportunity came along that would make him his own boss. Ironically, I first came in contact with him in a situation where his ambition and abilities were being totally frustrated.

Joe Kohler graduated from Cornell University with a degree in hotel management, class of 1971. He was born and raised in ski country. He had an early aptitude for skiing and became a ski instructor while still in college. Cornell recommended him for a position as managing director of

JOSEPH KOHLER, *founder and CEO, Ski View, Inc.*

the Windham Mountain Club, in Windham, New York. I was a member of the board of governors. We owned the mountain and the board did its best to duplicate the atmosphere of a private golf club with the usual social amenities.

Unfortunately, Kohler was given responsibility without the necessary authority; an impossible situation. He was only twenty-two, but it was easy (for me, at least) to spot the fact that Joe was a winner, despite his diffidently respectful manner.

Tom Sheridan bought Windham Mountain and developed it as a commercial ski area. It had been losing money, so he formed a club, and a group of investors became its charter members. Sheridan was a bright, well-connected lawyer, but unfortunately did not have a great talent for administration. Besides, he had a full-time law practice. Nevertheless, he was paid to function as the club's chief executive officer. Kohler served as the chief operating officer.

Deficits were high, because there just weren't enough members. Eventually, the board of governors suggested that Tom resign. Then, despite my pleading, Kohler was passed over for the top job in favor of a retired Army colonel, John Meyer. The colonel was tall, handsome, and well-spoken, but I knew intuitively that he wouldn't make it—military training doesn't necessarily groom soldiers for business— and it hadn't in this case. If Kohler had been given a free hand, I am certain he would have rounded up the additional membership the club needed to be self-sufficient, which is exactly what he proceeded to do in his next situation.

In any case, Kohler resigned to become the managing director of the Bristol Mountain ski area in New York State's Adirondacks. Joe was not only executive director of the ski area, but two years later became president of its real-estate development company. The owner of the mountain, a Lebanese by the name of Sarkis, had raised his needed capital from forty-two shareholders. As the new president of the real-estate company, Joe also negotiated an equity position as part of his employment package. He stayed with Bristol Mountain from 1975 to 1981 and was highly successful. When he became Bristol's managing director, it was losing money. With Kohler in charge, they made money four years out of six (two years having been without snow). Joe had become a knowledgeable, aggressive marketing man who also developed a flair for finance. He negotiated $2.5 million in nonrecourse loans from the Farmers Home Administration and the Small Business Administration. He resigned his full-time position in 1981 to start his own business. He named it See and Ski. But he continued to work part-time developing Bristol's real-estate holdings, since he still had a 30 percent interest. It is the See and Ski business that this story is about, and here's how it came to pass.

In the spring of 1981, Kohler received a phone call from a Canadian company. They wanted to put advertising signs on the back of each ski-lift chair on Bristol Mountain. Joe rejected the idea because it offended his sense of aesthetics—too many signs. However, upon subsequent reflection, he saw there might be a basis for a new business using a different and considerably less expensive approach.

Aside from his "environmental" objection, Kohler thought the number of people reached by such a placement would be too few, it being visible *only* to the person riding the lift in the following chair. Then he thought, Why not create a much larger sign and put one on each of the *towers* that hold up the ski-lift cables? Those signs would be visible to *all* the skiers, and each sign would add a "Ski Safely" message. Joe had come up with an *important twist* on the idea that he had rejected. Bravo! Yet another moneymaking idea was born.

Because the mind of man is so fertile, the flow of new ideas and concepts seems to be endless. New ideas are out there just waiting to be embraced. Careful now, because we know that four out of five of those "wonderful" new ideas will die in the crib. Entrepreneurs must be smart enough, or lucky enough, to discard—or, as Kohler did, modify—ideas that possess a fundamental flaw.

Kohler had become president of the Ski Owners Association of New York State. He had also been elected to the board of directors of the Eastern Seaboard Ski Areas, as well as becoming a member of the governor's new Tramway Council. The council made recommendations on safety for all ski areas in the state. Joe, who had been passed over at Windham, was now obviously a young man on the rise. Although still in his mid-twenties, he was already seen as an industry leader.

The Canadian company had hoped to make Bristol its opening point for the U.S. market, because of Kohler's industry connections. It had offered Bristol $20,000 in annual rent for the right to place advertisements on the backs of every ski chair. After Kohler turned down the Canadian offer, he set to work in earnest to develop his own concept. He remembered having seen the Burma Shave roadside signs on childhood trips to Florida and felt they would be the perfect size and shape to put on the ski towers—about eighteen inches by thirty inches.

Joe was sure that most ski areas would welcome the cash, and the ads too, because in addition to being tasteful, each ad would promote ski safety. Thus, the benefit would be two-fold: a subliminal safety message and much-needed additional revenue. He and an architect designed an aesthetically pleasing, brown metal frame that would be permanently attached to each tower. The sign itself could then be changed easily as needed.

His first customer was Eastman Kodak, based in Rochester, New York. Kohler wrote the slogan, "Picture Yourself Skiing Safely—Kodak." A condiment maker was next after Kohler wrote, "Leave the Hotdogging to Us—French's Mustard." He put his own personality and cleverness into those first slogans (uncovering a talent he never knew he had), and he made the rounds of all the companies and the ski areas in New York ski country. Bristol Mountain alone had fifty-two towers to sell. A friend who managed a neighboring mountain signed up at once. To cover his up-front costs, Kohler needed to sell a hundred tower ads immediately.

In the beginning, Joe had no staff other than his Bristol Mountain staff. He was a one-man show, writing the advertisements, selling the companies on the idea of advertising, contacting ski areas to contract for additional ski lifts, and the day-to-day administration of the business.

He knew as little about the advertising business as I originally knew about the shirt business. Nor had he any knowledge of setting rate structure. He based his charges on the price the Canadian company had been willing to pay Bristol Mountain. As pricing strategies go, it was rather simplistic, $800 for each sign installed. His costs seemed to be modest: $50 for the board materials, a $200 fee for the mountain, and $120 for the advertising agency. On paper, it would appear that he would have a healthy profit. In actuality, he had not taken into account the research and development costs for the bracket system, nor the time and expense involved in selling the space to advertisers and in turn selling the ski areas to lease him their towers.

His first season, 1981, turned out to be a financial disaster: sales of $150,000; operating loss of $180,000. Joe had concentrated on local advertisers, many of whom did not renew for the second season. The costs for signing up the ski resorts *and* the advertisers were high—too high. Direct mail turned out to be ineffective. Personal sales calls were the only way to sign up either a ski area or an advertiser.

I liked the way Joe started his business—doing everything himself. He worked very hard, and frankly, he had been inspired. However, the problems in this new, real world began to wear him down. When he came to see me, I questioned the need for taking in partners, because management control might become a problem, but mainly because profits would have to be shared. Joe felt he had no choice. He couldn't keep See and Ski alive one more season without a substantial inflow of capital.

Kohler was desperate for financial help. His personal net worth was approximately $50,000. So he looked around for outside investors. And in the process he hooked up with two of the better minds in advertising—Martin Stern and Steve Blacker.

New advertising contacts, advertisers, and credibility in the form of a media research study were provided by Stern, then a senior account executive at Wells, Rich, Greene, one of the country's top agencies. He supplied the advertising expertise and practical business knowledge necessary for the fledgling company to take off. Stern also introduced Kohler to Blacker—formerly publisher of the *Village Voice*, the *New York Post*, and *Cue* magazine. Steve set up a more realistic rate card for the advertising and wrote the first media kit. The three partners changed the name of the company from See and Ski to Ski View.

One outside investor provided Kohler with a $500,000 line of credit in exchange for a 34 percent ownership in the corporation. (I would have bargained for 25 percent.) Joe now had his capital requirements taken care of. Both Stern and Blacker became minority shareholders in Ski View, the new corporation. Martin, Steve, and Joe wrote the first business plan and selected a strategic direction for the company.

The management team agreed with the advice given by a friend from Windham days, Norman B. Norman, founder of a well-known advertising agency—Norman, Craig & Kummel. Norman also had been a member of Windham's board of governors. He said that the new venture's expansion must be fast—very fast. As the idea could not be copyrighted, their only hope for success would be to enter all ski markets at once to discourage the large outdoor advertising companies from entering into competition.

The first national advertisers delivered by Martin Stern were Hiram Walker and Pontiac. And since they were now in the "big league," production requirements also changed. National advertisers demanded four-color printing, and production costs went up sharply.

The $500,000 new capital was used to cover the $180,000 first-year loss, the increased production costs, and to underwrite the cost of an in-house sales force to open both new advertising accounts and new ski-area accounts. It turned out to be the right move. Over the next four years, the company sold $16 million in advertising space.

Then in 1984, only three years after he started the business, Kohler and his partners sold Ski View for $7.3 million to Allegheny Media, a large national outdoor advertising firm. Joe's personal share of those proceeds was $2.5 million. And, the four original investors retained an equity position in the new company.

Since then, Kohler has formed a new company, as you might expect, this time with Rob Kircher: Target Media. The new business is selling time to local and national advertisers on closed-circuit television programming in hotel rooms. Target Media has not been in business long enough to judge its success. But Joe is confident that Target Media has a bigger future than Ski View. Time will tell, but in the meantime, to have earned a cool $2.5 million before turning thirty is not bad at all. Especially as he still has an equity position in the company he sold.

# 7

■ □ ■

# JULIAN BRODIE
## Expert Counseling for the New Retiree Market, at Wholesale

S uccess breeds success—sometimes. The experience and confidence obtained in managing a successful first career can usually be drawn on when developing a business of one's own. Case in point: Julian Brodie.

About thirty years ago, I played a fair amount of tennis with Julian. He is a good-looking, pleasant man, several years younger than I. We were out of touch for many years until recently when I ran into him and his wife Isabel at the theater.

I remembered hearing that he had retired from the advertising business in 1971, and said, "Well, Julian, how have you enjoyed your retirement?" And he replied, "Mortimer, you just don't keep up. I didn't retire, I started a new business."

In the current frenzy of mergers and acquisitions, many high-level executives have lost their jobs. Interestingly, it is anticipated that this free-lance managerial talent, still ambitious (and in many cases funded with generous sev-

JULIAN BRODIE (right), *founder and president, Retirement Program Services, pictured here with Richard Rodgers and Celeste Holm.*

erance packages), will become a new breed of mid-life entrepreneurs who will launch new businesses of their own.

Julian could well serve as their model, though in his case,
the mother of invention was necessity of a highly personal
nature. Problems within his own family led to his starting
a business to show other people how to avoid the pitfalls
of retirement and, to the extent humanly possible, diminish
the perils of aging.

The tennis court is not the best place to gather biograph-
ical information, so at lunch, following the theater outing
by a few days, I was surprised to learn that Julian had been
a child prodigy. He had entered New York University at the
age of thirteen—the youngest of the 37,000 students en-
rolled at the time—and was only seventeen when he received his B.A.

His father and two older brothers were in advertising, so
it was not altogether surprising that this prodigy began writing ads for a local menswear store when he was only fourteen. It was natural for him to enter that field following
college, and he did so with considerable success, eventually
emerging as a senior vice president at one of the world's
largest agencies.

But it was happenstance that led him into opening a business of his own. A family situation had developed requiring
special handling. Julian's mother and Isabel's mother and
father, having turned eighty, all found themselves unable
to cope with living on their own. It appeared they would
have to be resettled in nursing homes. Julian's home was
large enough to accommodate all three senior citizens. "I
decided to turn over our entire second floor. It had its own
separate entrance." He hired a housekeeper just for them
and opened what Julian dubbed his "geriatric country club."

Brodie saw, all too soon, how *inadequately* these three
people, so dear to him and his wife, had been prepared for

retirement. In today's world, the problems of retirement have been smoothed considerably by Social Security, Medicare, and corporate pension-plan programs. But it was plain to Julian that money covered only *one* aspect of the retirement problem; much, much more was needed. As he said to the family doctor, "You fellows are great at keeping old people alive, but you don't tell us what to *do* with them. But on second thought, that's really not a medical problem; it's a social problem."

And that's how it came about that he conceived his new idea, as sound as it is simple. Corporate employers should offer *preretirement* counseling programs to their personnel. Here are excerpts from our conversation. It spells out the need and the way his company would fill that need. Julian began selling me!

"Mortimer, you've been in business fifty years. Haven't you sometimes wondered about some of your employees who have given years, or maybe all of their business lives, to your company and who will shortly find themselves at liberty? Few retirees have been adequately prepared—mentally, emotionally, programmatically, or even budgetwise —to face this complete change in their lives and lifestyles. Most avoid even thinking about it. Or they brush it aside with the fond notion that they're now going to stay home and sleep, or 'play golf every day.' Many are unwittingly heading for what is becoming known as 'retirement shock.'

"It's an old adage—but one honored more in the breach than in the observance—that 'you shouldn't retire from something, but *to* something.' Not many really know how."

Brodie went on to explain that while financial packages had made early retirement more attractive, new corporate procedures were needed to prepare retiring personnel for life after work.

At this point he quoted from the brochure that is part of his presentation:

"Winston Churchill said, 'You can measure the civilization of a people by the way they treat their old folks.' And a White House Conference on the Aging said, 'Every employer has a major responsibility for providing preparation-for-retirement programs during their working hours.'

"My company is set up with a professional staff to do just that on corporate premises. You presumably have spent millions on your pension plans but not ten cents on preparing your retirees. And my plan would cost you peanuts. I have a staff of twenty-three professionals uniquely trained and thoroughly experienced in their individual specialties to help newly retired people handle the problems *and* the privileges of retirement."

I asked Julian how much it cost to get his company started. How did he go about it, and where did he get the money?

"Research, recruitment, training and program formulation took fourteen months," he told me. "It cost me three hundred twenty-five thousand dollars [in 1971 dollars]. I wasn't ready to solicit business until I had everything set up the way it should be.

"Today, thousands of 'enrollees' later, my counselors have all the up-to-date material plus well-developed techniques for involving and motivating older employees to *act* in their own interests.

"Few company investments these days meet so pressing a need for such a relatively small expenditure. One corporate client really wrote my copy: 'We're funding millions of dollars every year for retirement. Your service certainly seems well justified if we're to make our pension and retirement plans do the job they're intended to do. And why should we attempt to do it ourselves? It really is a job for pros.' "

Brodie had conceived an idea that meets my criterion of offering a service potential clients could go nowhere else to find. How exactly did he go about executing it? He was no expert on the problems of aging. But of course he was bright, and his advertising background had made him knowledge-able about marketing and about market research. He took the following steps.

He assembled a group of specialists who could address the individual problems all retirees face: pension options; figuring and balancing retirement income and outgo; wise money management, including changing insurance and investment objectives; tax savings; postretirement paid-work opportunities; opportunities in volunteer work; whether and where to relocate; the mental and physical health of the retiree; travel and avocational guidance.

These experts agreed to serve as his Advisory Council. They were knowledgeable in their specialties, though no one in those days had concentrated his specialty on the areas of *preretirement*. They agreed there was a need for such a service (and most have been serving on the council ever since).

He researched the market possibilities by creating a presentation that he and a free-lance researcher showed to sixty-two large corporations. They asked two simple questions: (1) Did the corporation believe there was a need for such a service? (2) If they agreed that there was a need, would they want Julian to return when his service was ready to be offered? Sixty of the sixty-two corporations said yes on both counts.

Armed with these results, Brodie launched his new company, Retirement Program Services. He put together a small group of investors (that seemed to be no problem; everyone liked his idea) and set up handsome headquarters in the Newsweek Building on Madison Avenue at Fiftieth Street, a prime midtown Manhattan location. He had well-furnished seminar rooms, several chambers for individual consultations, a library, a gallery, and a houseman to serve coffee, etc. Julian had assumed that corporations would confine the privilege of his services to middle and top management, off corporate premises.

Now then, here's the joker. As I said earlier, one can research the market for a new business quite thoroughly and reach conclusions that are 95 percent correct. However, one frequently fails to learn about that *unknown* 5 percent; and in Brodie's case, he learned about it late, though not too late.

After spending his precious seed money on impressive headquarters, Brodie discovered that he didn't need that setup at all. His clients wanted the seminars and the counseling to be conducted on their *own* corporate premises. Furthermore, they wanted a more modest program so that *all* preretirement employees would be offered the retirement counseling.

A moment's reflection makes this reasoning easy to understand. Conducting retirement seminars on corporate premises would create a highly visible employee benefit, with the corporation itself as the benefactor. The fact that the corporation cared enough to offer professional help and guidance on life *after* retirement was certain to be an enormous builder of good will.

When Julian was telling his story, I had interrupted to ask, "Why would you need investors?" I had started my business with $2,000, never thinking to have either a partner or an investor. And I had thought that Brodie would begin by conducting the seminars himself and slowly adding staff as the business required.

Brodie explained that he was not a specialist but a generalist. He needed a staff of experts, because his service, as he had conceived it, would consist of six to nine seminars, each seminar covering a different aspect of retirement. Each seminar was to be conducted by a specialist in that particular field, and his literature made that quite plain.

If it had been my business and if I had thought to research the market, I believe that ten or fifteen companies would have given me all the confirmation I would have needed. Yet, Julian was probably smart to have conducted his broader survey, because that was certain to give investors the confidence necessary to put up money. But I would not have set up such elaborate headquarters. Just think how much that little "5 percent mistake" cost him. First, most of that $325,000 was wasted. Second, and of much greater importance, instead of keeping all that profit for himself, he was obliged to share it with his investors. If he had done it my way, I believe he could have started the business entirely on his own, borrowing nothing. However, that is only conjecture.

But then, it is to be expected that every entrepreneur will make mistakes in the beginning. The important thing here is that Brodie's underlying idea was so sound. There was a real need for his services. Fortunately, he rented his headquarters at a time when New York City real estate costs were at an all-time low. His space was $16 per square foot; today that space would cost $55 per square foot. So he had no trouble subletting the space at a profit.

It's not really important to the story to know exactly what Brodie's present net income is. Suffice it to say he's been in the business for fifteen years and continues to drive new Jaguars. I probably could estimate his annual income to within $100,000, but it's not really that important. What matters is that Julian saw a need, created an answer to that need, did some impressive marketing research, prepared an appropriately simple presentation, drew on the wisdom of a carefully chosen council, established the financial backing, and recruited the necessary personnel.

Brodie started life as a child prodigy and remains a prodigy as a senior citizen, with enviable vim and vigor. "It's the usefulness of our services that makes my work a pleasure and keeps my batteries charged," he told me. "I am one lucky man." And indeed he is.

# 8

### KENNETH JAY LANE
### An Eye for Fashion Trends
### Finds a Gold Mine in
### Rhinestones

Kenneth Jay Lane is a good-looking *bon vivant*, the perfect image of a man about town with a matching man-about-town charm. He has a luscious, old-world apartment on Park Avenue with a huge living room and sixteen-foot ceilings. The feeling of this splendid room seemed to me to reveal the influence of Lady Mendl, the famous decorator who reigned in the 1920s and 1930s. As it turns out, Denning & Fourcade of London created the interior with Lane himself the main inspiration for the look.

A life-size portrait of Lane at the age of twenty-one hangs on one wall. In it, he is Rudolph Valentino and Ramon Novarro rolled into one. He was one gorgeous young man, and he has matured into a handsome and still relatively lean man.

How did it come about that Kenny (as his friends call him) became an internationally famous designer and manufacturer of costume jewelry for the beautiful people? Lane's

KENNETH JAY LANE, *president, Kenneth Jay Lane, Inc.*

entrepreneurial success is the story of an artistic talent that found its expression in a surprising commercial form: diamonds, emeralds, pearls, rubies, and sapphires—all fake. His education was in taste, not in business. Yet today he sells $20 million worth of costume jewelry annually in his own shops (five, at last count) and in upscale stores here and abroad. How it all came about is a revealing study of creativity in the fashion marketplace.

That he started his own business was due entirely to happenstance. However, he did have an aptitude for fashion—an eye for beautiful design. And he was so handsome and personable that he moved with ease into the exclusive circles of high fashion. In this milieu, he received an education that was the equivalent of a Harvard M.B.A. for the conventional businessman. Kenny's talent was not immediately apparent. He earned his B.A. at the University of Michigan. There his interest in the arts was sparked by fellow student Frank O'Hara, a poet and writer who would gain considerable fame. Incidentally, at the age of nineteen, I too met a mentor of sorts in the person of Victor Edward Thal III. (I subsequently found out that the "III" was a cover to hide a middle-class background.) Victor was a painter who had hobnobbed with Hemingway in Paris. He opened my eyes to literature and art, two subjects that had been missing in my life, due, I suppose, to the circles in which I moved and my scanty formal education.

In any event, Lane couldn't wait to escape the Midwest ("Go East, Young Man"). His father owned an auto-supply business, and his mother worked as a U.S. marshal. Kenny knew he had to break away. He used the Rhode Island School of Design as his excuse. Then, at twenty-one, through a series of fortuitous introductions, he gained entry to the art departments of the country's two most prestigious fashion magazines, *Vogue* and *Harper's Bazaar*.

"Introductions were never a problem for me," Lane recalls, and that is an understatement, for Kenny charms old friends and perfect strangers with equal facility. A friend, Carrie Donovan, herself a recent graduate of Parsons School of Design, introduced him to Alexander Liberman, the brilliant art director at *Vogue*, and not too long after, he met Alexey Brodovitch, the art director at *Harper's Bazaar*. He was offered summer jobs at both magazines. He decided on *Vogue*, even though the famous Diana Vreeland was editor of *Harper's Bazaar* at the time. He was only a staff assistant in the art department, but he liked it enough that, at summer's end, he talked a full-timer in the department to quit to pursue her interest in a nursing career. He stayed at *Vogue* for another year, working as an assistant to the merchandising director, Elisa Daggs. When Elisa left the magazine in 1956, Kenny, out of respect for their relationship, left also.

As luck would have it, he met, at one of the innumerable parties he went to, Roger Vivier, the premier shoe designer for Dior in Paris and Delman in New York. Roger, in turn, introduced him to Josephi, Delman's shoe designer, who hired him as an assistant.

Genesco, a large and at that time successful conglomerate, acquired Delman Shoes in 1958, and Kenny received an invitation to study shoe design in Paris with Dior. When he tendered his resignation to Maxey Jarman, chairman of Genesco, Maxey convinced him to turn down the Dior job and stay with Genesco as a sort of fashion scout. Six months of the year he would spend in Paris sending weekly fashion reports to Maxey, and the other six months integrating some of the European influence into Genesco's various businesses. To put it another way, Kenny was to be Genesco's overall stylist. Kenny accepted the offer.

That sublime situation lasted two years, from 1959 to 1961. Kenny had almost carte blanche to entertain, with a liberal expense account to back it up. In addition, he himself was wined and dined to a fare-thee-well because of Genesco's enormous buying power in shoes and clothing for men and women.

Lane made the job out to be frivolous in our conversation, but it sharpened his eye for trends. His weekly letter informed Maxey what the beautiful people were doing and wearing, but it also trained Kenny to be quick in spotting new trends in the world of fashion.

Because of his flair for style (and despite the fact that he was not a technician), Lane unofficially became Delman's shoe designer, modifying the couture shoes of Dior into less extreme American styles.

Then in 1963 an incident occurred that led to the beginning of Kenneth Jay Lane Costume Jewelry. The well-known American designer Scaasi (Isaacs, the designer's real name, spelled backward) was at the height of his popularity. Genesco was supplying Scaasi with ladies' shoes to match his new gowns. Evening shoes, at that time, were often decorated with rhinestones. A suggestion was made that Lane make matching rhinestone buttons, and Kenny, on his own, added earrings and bracelets to match the buttons. The jewelry was large, but light in weight. "They sparkled plenty," Kenny said.

A company called Accessocraft had the license to manufacture Scaasi jewelry. When Kenny suggested that they make his pieces part of their Scaasi line, they declined, saying the jewelry wasn't commercial. But the *New York Times* heard about the bracelets and sparkly earrings and sent fashion editor Pat Peterson to interview Lane. Kenny had to list some store as a source of the merchandise, so he named Bonwit Teller, a fully owned subsidiary of Genesco. When the story appeared, the Bonwit Teller jewelry buyer ordered a dozen pairs of the matching sets; they sold out in five minutes, a subsequent two dozen sold out in ten minutes. At this point, the earrings were handmade with rhinestones that had been extracted from bracelets purchased at the local five-and-dime stores. Although the rhinestones were the same, Kenny's designs made them seem totally different.

Happenstance also played a role in the enthusiastic reception Lane's jewelry received. This was a time when women of high fashion had turned away from wearing their diamonds because of the resurgence in jewel thefts. And it actually became the in-thing to wear *faux bijoux*.

Two months later, Eugenia Sheppard, the *Times* fashion columnist, did a feature on Kenny and his jewelry, and that started a veritable stampede. Lane received phone calls from most of the country's better stores. Within a short while, his jewelry was in these stores coast-to-coast. Because three of those stores—Bonwit Teller, Henri Bendel, and Giddings-Jenny—were owned by Genesco, Lane decided he should resign his position with the parent company. His sales to the stores soon exceeded his salary as shoe designer, in any case. Thus, Kenneth Jay Lane, Inc., was on its way.

With an outlet for his creativity in place, Lane soon conceived another unusual concept. The idea came to him while riding a bus to a shoe factory that had retained him as a free-lance designer. It was to cover bracelets with cobra skin, using the same technique that shoe manufacturers use to cover the heel of a lady's shoe. The cobra bracelets proved to be as popular as the rhinestone earrings.

From his Paris days, Kenny remembered that Marella Agnelli (wife of Fiat's chairman, Gianni Agnelli) dressed simply but with one arm covered with snake bracelets. He borrowed that design concept, replacing her valuable turquoise stones with imitation turquoise beads, and thus was born his famous animal bracelet series. He did the same thing with seashell jewelry, inspired by the international jeweler Fulco di Verdura's encrusting shells with diamonds and other gems, and that was followed by Kenny's enamel bracelets.

Lane also thoroughly understood the retail-industry mentality, insight gained by his experiences at Genesco. He never went over a buyer's head, even though socially he was on a first-name basis with the operating heads of many major department stores.

The money flowed in, and Kenny, having been well briefed on the elegant life during his stay in Paris, set up his sumptuous town house in New York where he entertained friends, clients, and the press with charming lunches and dinners, mixing gourmet food and guests with the skill of a born host. His creations graced numerous covers of *Harper's Bazaar* and *Vogue*, and he appeared on television frequently. Each exposure spurred new interest, inquiries, and sales. So his business grew and prospered.

In 1983, Lane opened his first retail store in New York's glittering Trump Tower on Fifth Avenue. That boutique is a tiny 135 square feet, and grossed $500,000 in its third year. That is $3,700 per square foot—a figure that belongs in *Ripley's Believe It or Not*. The success encouraged him to open a second store on Columbus Avenue, the West Side's new yuppie quarter, and that was followed by a large store on Rodeo Drive in Beverly Hills. As of this writing, plans are being drawn for shops in San Francisco and Dallas.

Kenny plans to expand his line to include handbags and belts as a hedge against the fickle tastes of the American consumer. His "lemons" have been few and far between, because he believes in classic designs. His line ranges in price from $30 to $300, with some "jeweled" belts costing up to $500.

There was a short period in the late 1970s when costume jewelry temporarily lost its appeal. It was a time when gold shot up in value from $35 to $900 an ounce, and women began buying gold jewelry as an investment. Because of rising prices, the "real thing" took on an additional allure. Fortunately, Lane survived, because the price of gold dropped sharply, and at the moment there is no holding him back. All this from one rhinestone button.

# 9
∎ ☐ ∎

# STEW LEONARD
## Selling Milk and Groceries in a "Magic Kingdom" Setting

An entrepreneur's taste and aptitudes often combine to make the business he creates uniquely his own. Such is the case with fifty-three-year-old Stew Leonard. He is the founder and owner of a unique kind of supermarket. His business is in a class by itself, because it is *not* exactly a supermarket. The emporium, with its broad one-way aisle snaking counterclockwise through the merchandise (so customers are forced to pass by every product offered) is located in the modest, partly blue-collar town of Norwalk, Connecticut, population 80,000. Yearly sales, in that one store, amount to $80 million—more, I have been given to understand, than any other single food store in the entire country. The store carries only 600 items (compared with 14,000 in a typical supermarket), yet draws customers from all over the New York metropolitan area.

To meet Stew Leonard is to like him, immediately. He

STEW LEONARD, *founder and owner, Stew Leonard's*

radiates good health, and total pleasure in the joy of living. His laughing eyes crinkle up when he smiles, and he smiles readily.

Like most entrepreneurs, Leonard was born with an undiluted desire "to be somebody." Being the sixth of seven children, it was always, "Stew, get this; Stew, get that." And from Stew: "Can I go with you?" with the reply being, "Yes, if you . . ."

Leonard's father was a milkman, and for those of you who don't know (I certainly didn't), this is what a milkman did. Charles Leonard bought milk in forty-quart cans from a local farmer, pasteurized it, bottled it, and then delivered it early in the morning to the homes of his customers, along with butter, cream, and eggs. When Stew was young, his father made deliveries in a horse-drawn wagon.

Leonard idolized his father and wanted nothing more than to do exactly what his father was doing. He spent as much time as he could on the milk route with his dad, even though that meant getting up at 3 A.M.

A milk route meant being in business for oneself, but it was really nothing more than a hard way of making a fair-to-middling living. Milk routes were bought and sold in the same way that local dry-cleaning stores, laundromats, and stationery stores keep changing hands.

Leonard attended the University of Connecticut's School of Agriculture, working toward a degree in dairy manufacturing, but dropped out in 1951 after his second year. His father had been forced to retire after suffering two heart attacks. Stew and his brother Jim took over the family business, which by then consisted of four milk routes known collectively as Clover Farms Dairy. Stew's dad died later that year, and the entire business was appraised at $21,000.

From 1951 to 1959, the dairy was run by Leonard and his brother with very little change. Stew enjoyed people, and he enjoyed selling, so it was natural for him to enroll with Dale Carnegie. He took these courses quite seriously, and was particularly interested in marketing angles. At a New York City trade fair, he found a man who made fiberglass figures. Stew ordered four cows' heads that he put on the roof of each of his milk trucks, plus one whole cow that he put on the back of the open truck he used for a family vehicle. When children waved, the driver pushed a button, and the cows would say, "Moo." Clover Farms Dairy became even more widely known. This penchant for showmanship helped him later on. It seems like such a small thing, yet it was important, because it added a light touch to the nitty-gritty of business.

In 1963, brother Jim decided to retire from the milk-route business, and Leonard bought him out. He continued operating his milk routes until 1967 when circumstances turned his business upside down. There were three factors at work:

1. Since most homes now had refrigerators, there was really no longer any *need* to have milk delivered daily. Customer loyalty only went so far, and Stew realized that the milkman was going the way of the iceman.

2. A new kind of competitor, Cumberland Farms, had opened eight "convenience stores" in the region, selling butter, eggs, cream, and milk at discount prices. Cumberland Farms sold a half-gallon of milk for 49 cents; Stew's delivered price was 69 cents. Cumberland Farms was cash-and-carry; Stew had charge accounts; so it was not surprising that his prices were so much higher and he was fast losing customers to Cumberland.

3. When the Connecticut Turnpike, Interstate 95, was approved, Leonard's property and dairy plant were con-

demned. The condemnation was generous; the state paid him about $200,000. However, after paying his lawyer, his taxes and mortgage, he netted only $70,000. (That was a hard pill to swallow.) But he no longer had a business, his old milk route having become an anachronism.

Leonard now had $70,000, and he was still highly motivated. He actually visited forty-three other dairies across the country to see if there were any further possibilities for him in the dairy business. But he saw that even the big dairies were having their troubles. Supermarket chains (like A & P) were by-passing commercial dairies and building their own milk-processing plants. This meant Leonard could no longer even consider the possibility of building a plant to sell wholesale. And he certainly could not rely on the continuation of his home-delivery routes.

Back home again in Connecticut, a friend told him about a man who was selling milk at discount prices directly from his own farm. Bernie Gouz of Hempstead, Long Island, was doing, shall we say, a land-office business on his land by selling milk at only 42 cents a half-gallon. Stew went to the farm, introduced himself, and asked for permission to watch this phenomenon. Gouz had no objection, and subsequently, the two men became good friends.

Leonard, a dedicated marketing man, spent three days in Gouz's parking lot asking customers why they were buying from Gouz instead of buying at the supermarket. The research served him well. The answer seemed to be that Gouz's milk was fresher (they could watch it being bottled right there). And, of course, the price was right. They didn't think the supermarket milk was as fresh. You could see Gouz's milk because it was packaged in glass bottles. In supermarkets, milk was sold in paper cartons.

And that's how the whole thing started. Leonard thought he would do the same thing in his own hometown, but with a *modest* variation. He had learned two things. People bought from Gouz because (1) they could see the milk being bottled on the premises and believed it to be fresher than supermarket milk; and (2) they were getting the lowest possible price because, obviously, they were buying it directly from the manufacturer—that is, the milk was being processed before their very eyes.

Stew decided to do exactly what Gouz had done *except* that he would bring the farm to "Main Street," the Boston Post Road (the original route from New York to Boston that parallels the Connecticut Turnpike). Leonard bought three acres of farmland with a hundred feet directly on the Post Road. The traffic count there was 22,000 cars a day.

Hazel Schultz, the widow who sold him the three acres, wondered what she would do with her animals, and Stew said, "Don't worry; I'll take them." That was Walt Disney talking. I should point out that in addition to the respect he had for his dad, Leonard had endless admiration for what Disney had accomplished in his career. Stew had actually gone out of his way to visit and explore Disneyland twice.

Leonard planned to set up a miniature farm to entertain his customers' children. There would be goats, chickens, sheep, cows, a small stream, a waterfall, and a water wheel using recirculating water.

Stew talked his plan over with Phil Baker, a neighbor who owned a successful Norwalk restaurant. Baker told Stew that he could apply for and would undoubtedly get a substantial loan from a local bank that would be guaranteed by the Small Business Administration. Leonard applied for and received a $492,500 loan at 4.75 percent interest from the Merchants Bank in Norwalk.

Like most entrepreneurs, Leonard also made mistakes.

He was sales-oriented, never money-oriented. Balance sheets, projected sales, markup, cash flow—all were a foreign language that held little interest. "If I take care of my customers, my customers will take care of me. To this day, I don't want to get involved in financial management; I don't even like to talk about it." And he didn't.

He told his architect, Dick Bergmann, that he wanted everything to be the best quality. His dairy store had to look like a farm. Bergmann suggested asphalt shingles for the roof, and Stew insisted they be wood, and this fidelity to quality and authenticity was to be carried throughout. The architect's first rendering showed a dairy that Stew felt looked more like a church than a farm. Leonard turned to another friend, Joe Shaw, a graphic artist. Over lunch, Shaw used his napkin to sketch his idea of a dairy farm. Stew's architect agreed on the more farmlike image, and redrew his plans for a more rustic farm building. In this case, the taste of the entrepreneur was the valid criterion, not the expertise of the professional.

The building itself was expensive, too expensive. And then Leonard had to install and pay for the latest automatic milk-processing equipment, including stacking machines, conveyors, and packaging machines—all shining chrome against gleaming white tiles. So the $70,000 cash from the sale of his land and the $492,500 SBA loan were not enough. An additional $600,000 loan obtained from Ray Peterson, his equipment supplier, was also soon dissipated. (It must be obvious that neither Stew nor I was really qualified to start our own business.) And Stew still had to stock his store. He prevailed upon his major suppliers of eggs, butter, and cheese to give him credit for seven weeks. He would use the money generated from seven weeks' sales as his much-needed working capital. They agreed because of Leonard's determination and enthusiasm. There was also the fact that Stew had not incorporated the business, which would have provided him with some measure of personal security. The suppliers admired him for putting everything he had in the world "on the line." Stew's wife Marianne cosigned every note.

Leonard opened his Clover Farms Dairy store in 1969. He was swamped with business for three reasons:

1. The spotlessly clean, brilliantly chromed milk-processing plant was visible through the spotlessly clean, plate-glass windows, and customers could watch fresh milk actually being packaged. People bought the freshly packaged milk as it left the conveyor belt. What a gimmick!

2. The ridiculously low prices; Stew was actually selling eggs at a loss. He had projected sales of 100 cases of eggs a week; he was selling 500 cases a week. Because of his seven-week line of credit, he was able to generate a sizable and much-needed cash flow.

3. Show biz: a glass-enclosed dairy plant, live animals, a water wheel, and waterfalls—Disneyland for free, and discount prices to boot. People had fun shopping here.

Leonard was still offering only the same few products he had offered on his home-delivery routes: milk, eggs, butter, cream, plus orange juice, bread, cottage cheese, and sour cream—they being the same products stocked by his discount competitor, Cumberland Farms. He did not carry a complete supermarket line; he specialized. His pricing strategy was to sell all his products (except eggs) for the same price as Cumberland, but he emphasized quality, entertainment, and friendliness. His own sincere affection for his customers is passed down the line to all his employees. His store became famous overnight—all by word of mouth. The fact that he was selling eggs for *less* than wholesale spread like wildfire. And of course the store was unique; mothers, children in tow, flocked to him rather than Cumberland.

Since opening, Leonard has enlarged his store twenty-three different times! Following the success of his on-the-premises milk-processing, his daughter Beth opened her own bakery on the premises. The bakery specializes in croissants; chocolate-chip cookies; warm, fresh-from-the-oven rolls and bread; homemade corn and bran muffins; and doughnuts and pies. Once again, the secret is focusing on fewer items. The bakery sells less than 5 percent of the items sold in a normal "in-store bakery" but recently it was written up as being the largest "in-store bakery" in America, with sales of over $100,000 per week.

For three years, Leonard operated his store under the name of his dad's company, Clover Farms Dairy. Then in 1972 he changed the name to Stew Leonard's. That came about, really, because of his infatuation with Disney. He had observed, for instance, that "Stew Leonard" had the same number of syllables as "Walt Disney." Sheepishly, Stew discussed the change with brother Jim. He wanted badly to rename the store, but worried that he might appear egotistical or foolish. He was afraid too of the family's reaction. Jim said, "Go ahead," and Stew did, placing a huge new sign out front. Leonard knew, finally, that he had arrived. "I feel that my customers know I am there watching over the business. They might not have felt that had I continued with Clover Farms—too much like a large corporation. Imagine if Disneyland had been called 'Continental Amusement Parks'—it just wouldn't be the same."

When Leonard had been forced to make a sales projection to get his bank loan, he figured that he would need $1 million in annual sales volume to cover his interest payments and to leave something to live on. So he predicted

$250,000 in sales (the 1967 sales level) for the milk routes, plus $750,000 in sales at the dairy store. His actual sales far exceeded his expectations.

Despite his truly enormous sales, Stew has never been out of debt. Stew's financial adviser had pointed out the advantages of assuming debt: by borrowing money from his bank, his government, his equipment suppliers, and his produce suppliers, Stew was able to parlay the $70,000 from the sale of his land into a business that now generates almost $100 million in annual sales.

As of this writing, Leonard is working on a second location—in Danbury, Connecticut, about twenty-one miles from his present place, on the forty acres he recently bought there. Danbury, a once-thriving industrial community that came upon hard times when plants and mills moved south, received a much-needed lift in 1982 when Union Carbide selected it for its new world headquarters.

Leonard was most enthusiastic at the prospects for his new Danbury branch, because he would then have enough room to incorporate *all* of his Walt Disney ideas, ideas he could not execute in Norwalk because of space limitations. However, I pointed out that Danbury, being farther away from New York, had a smaller population to draw upon than his Norwalk store. He was momentarily taken aback. He hadn't given much thought to the demographics. He assumed the area would be right for him because a huge shopping center was being built on the acreage that had been used for the former Danbury Fair. I pointed out that people would travel fifteen or twenty miles to spend a morning or afternoon shopping, but they would not drive that far to buy milk, eggs, and groceries.

Stew Leonard is going ahead with the Danbury branch; however, local environmentalists have delayed the construction. Therefore, as of this writing, an answer as to the success of the new store is not known. But should Stew turn out to be wrong, he will have earned the right to be wrong.

Stew is lucky in having four children—Stew Jr., Tom, and Jill, in addition to Beth—who are all actively involved in the operation. Stew Jr. was named president this past year.

DEAN SLOANE, *president, C. P. Rehab Corporation*

# 10

■ □ ■

# DEAN SLOANE
## Delivering Sophisticated Health Care in a Profitable New Way

In recent years, law and accounting have been two professions from which successful entrepreneurs often spring, one might almost say escape. Dean Sloane, CPA, is such a man. Tall, elegantly turned out, and handsome, Dean looks like the kind of fellow who might easily have been cast in the role of seducer in silent films. But images can be deceiving. Dean is a first-rate, down-to-earth, sensitive man who understands business and is not afraid to work.

Sloane earned his B.A. in accounting at Ithaca (N.Y.) College, with a partial scholarship in baseball. Actually, he started out to be a professional ballplayer, a far cry from the way he ended up. His faculty adviser suggested that he switch from a B.S. in business administration to accounting, believing that accounting would be more useful, and it was. Dean went directly from college into Deloitte, Haskins & Sells, one of America's Big Eight accounting firms. By his third year, he had earned the status of senior accountant.

Somewhere along the line, Sloane decided that he would rather not pursue an accounting career. Then by chance a good friend, Salvatore Alternative (his real name), turned up with an alternative. At this point, Dean was twenty-seven and Sal was thirty-eight.

Alternative's background was investment banking, where he made a modest fortune which, as sometimes happens, he subsequently lost. Now he had come across an idea with a big potential. He helped raise capital for a Pennsylvania company, Rehab Corporation, that at the time had twelve branches offering medical care to people with heart problems. There were three groups of patients: those who had had open-heart surgery, those who'd had a heart attack, and those with stable angina.

Cardiac rehabilitation for each of these groups called for the kind of activity and supervision that was not readily available from practicing cardiologists.

This situation is particularly interesting because the idea was not Sloane's to begin with. In fact, it was not even Sal Alternative's idea. Alternative had arranged the financing for the Rehab Corporation, in return for which he was given a New York franchise. Alternative realized that he knew financing but nothing about administration. So it was Sloane who got the ball and carried it for a touchdown. Here's how it came about.

Alternative wanted a partner who would become the operating head of the new venture, because he lacked that aptitude and even the desire. Alternative knew he could raise the funds needed to open a chain of medical facilities, even though at the time the two of them had only $17,000 between them. Alternative also believed that Sloane would make a perfect partner. However, Dean needed considerable persuasion, because the new venture was complicated indeed, and in the beginning his salary would be next to nothing—$10,000. Eventually he made the decision: "I'll do it!"

People with heart disease need supervised exercise, diet, and medication. At a minimum, they require three months of close supervision to become conditioned to a permanent change in lifestyle, a change most difficult to make for the average person.

When Sloane was telling me the stories about his rehabilitation centers, I was somewhat skeptical about the effectiveness of all that exercising. But we recently had a dinner guest who, following open heart surgery, spent six months in one of Sloane's rehabilitation centers. Our friend Potter reported that the change in his physical condition had been extraordinary. When he first visited the rehabilitation center, he would get tired from walking just one block. Now he is back to playing tennis regularly, something he thought would never happen. If the rehabilitation centers can be this effective, it is small wonder that they have been so successful.

Anyway, Sloane's proposed cardiovascular centers would be a cooperative effort between the C. P. Rehab Corporation, managed by Dean Sloane, and groups of doctors who would take the responsibility for the medical supervision of the patients. Each cooperating doctor would recommend that his patients go to the center to effect the much-needed lifestyle change. Profits would be shared fifty-fifty between the medical corporation formed by the doctors and C. P. Rehab.

At the time, the projected costs to open a 2,000-square-foot center was $75,000. Each center would need a fair amount of sophisticated medical equipment. Alternative was able to secure a $500,000 loan from the Irving Trust Company. When I asked, "What was the basis for such a loan; how could the bank go out on a limb like that?" Sloane explained that the bank had the medical equipment as security, plus his own background as a senior accountant, and the example of the twelve branches already operating successfully in Pennsylvania.

The beginning, in 1973, was shaky for Sloane. Besides having to accept a $10,000 annual salary, a considerable comedown, there were really tough problems with the physicians about the basic concept. The average center would service about ten doctors, but it was almost impossible to convince the doctors that the two corporate partners were entitled to a fifty-fifty split. The doctors wanted an eighty-twenty split, with 80 percent going to the doctors. They had the medical training, they were supplying the patients, and they were responsible for the physical well-being of those patients who participated. There was a further problem. One doctor might be sending the center ten patients while another doctor would be sending only two patients, and yet they both would receive the same percentage out of their profits. By tradition, the doctors could not ethically (or legally) receive "commissions" based on the number of patients they recommended. So it is easy to see why negotiations were always so difficult. Negotiations were concluded, however, after they were shown the contract that had been signed. Besides, their patients would actually live longer, and the doctors would get additional income.

So there was always a problem in persuading a group of doctors to go into a partnership with his company, but Sloane was persuasive. His briefing went something like this: "I believe you will agree that you should offer, as a regular part of your practice, a cardiac rehabilitation service. You can't set it up for yourself, and before *we* can set up such a center, we will need ten doctors to join up with us. You would send us those patients who would benefit from such therapy. I will set up such a center, lease the equipment, rent the space, hire a manager and a staff who will supervise the entire operation. Your job is to send in the patients and see to it that our staff does right by your patients."

The doctors would form a medical corporation and elect one doctor to become president. The president of that corporation would be the main liaison between the medical staff and the business manager of C. P. Rehab. The patients would come to the facilities three times a week for up to six months. Three months should be the minimum.

Sloane, Alternative, and the doctors were persuaded of the efficacy of the treatment by the success of the Pennsylvania rehabilatation centers. This was a concept that had never existed up until that time: a corporate group of doctors merging with a management group to offer continuing treatment for heart patients. The cost to the patient was $2,500 for the first three months: About $200 a week. In contrast, a hospital room varies in price from $200 to $500 a day.

C. P. Rehab has since gone through a whole series of expansions, the first of which was in 1979. Sloane visited Florida for a short holiday and realized immediately that he was in a perfect market for their centers: all those retirees, many suffering from heart disease. He and Alternative went back to the Pennsylvania firm and arranged for an extension on their license so that they could open branches in Florida. After opening three centers there, they went back to Pennsylvania and bought out the entire franchising license. They could then open as many centers as they wanted, wherever they wanted. They thought Florida alone could handle twenty centers. To do that, however, they would need additional capital. In August of 1980, with Alternative's guidance, they raised $5 million through a public offering. There are currently sixty-five rehabilitation centers in fourteen states.

A hidden risk in their entire venture was the threat that

Medicare or the insurance companies might no longer cover the treatments they were offering. And although that risk was never realized, Dean decided to look into the possibility of diversifying. So in 1981 he came up with the bright idea of moving into the hospital market. They offered a cardio-pulmonary management system (CPMS) for computerized electrocardiography and other noninvasive cardiopulmo-nary procedures. Basically, C. P. Rehab would provide a cost-efficient alternative to hospitals, enabling them to offer sophisticated diagnostic services to their patients without the tremendous capital investment needed to buy the elab-orate medical and data-processing equipment. The testing and the necessary administrative support are all performed by CPMS employees. At this writing, they are running the noninvasive cardiac departments (their own franchises, really) in fourteen New York City hospitals. It has turned out to be a bonanza.

In the hospitals, once again, there is a partnership ar-rangement. The hospital revenue now represents 60 percent of Rehab's annual sales, and 75 percent of their after-tax profits. In 1981, before the corporation went public, sales were $1.8 million, with a $200,000 after-tax profit. Sales for 1986 were $31 million.

In a further hedging effort, Sloane came up with another idea, once again organizing a group of physicians. This time they would refer their patients to a testing lab, knowing that the lab would take no shortcuts. And because they would be partners, the doctors would also participate in some share of the profits. Their six diagnostic imaging cen-ters include the most up-to-date diagnostic imaging equip-ment for general radiology, fluoroscopy and tomography, ultrasound, mammography, CAT scanning, nuclear medi-cine, and digital angiography. The facilities also offer cardiac rehabilitation, stress-testing, holter-monitoring and nuclear cardiology. One center in Queens, New York, performs 25,000 outpatient diagnostic procedures annually, with sixty participating physicians. Dean expects this division to be the biggest part of their company within the next three years.

*Inc.* magazine publishes a list of the fastest-growing companies in the United States, called the Inc. 100. C. P. Rehab has been on that list for the last four years, and Dean hopes they will be the first company to make the list for five years running. Time will tell.

GLENN BERNBAUM, *founder and owner, Mortimer's restaurant*

# 11

■ □ ■

## GLENN BERNBAUM
### Snob Appeal Made
### Mortimer's the Playpen for
### the Rich and Famous

Restaurants come and go, many of them coming in with extravagent acclaim and going out in well-deserved obscurity. Even those that open to solid reviews frequently fail to sustain their appeal. It is a most volatile business and not recommended. The restaurateur who does not spend most of his waking hours on the premises usually can count on pilfered receipts, along with a sharp decline in quality and service. So it is a terribly demanding and time-consuming business as well—all in all, perhaps not an attractive option for the budding entrepreneur.

Yet a supremely successful restaurant may be instructive to look at for the manner in which it established its identity and an ambience that became even more appealing as the restaurant became older. Such a place is Mortimer's, located on Manhattan's fashionable Upper East Side. In the twelve years since it opened, it has become internationally famous, and heavily patronized by the beautiful people, thanks entirely to the single-minded approach of Glenn Bernbaum, the founder and owner. He favors only the beautiful people and gives short shrift to those who do not belong.

Mortimer's has given me more personal publicity than I've received at The Custom Shop throughout its fifty-year history. Glenn Bernbaum named it after me as a courtesy because I permitted Glenn to remain as my chief operating officer in spite of the time-consuming challenge of starting his new restaurant. He managed to handle both jobs for three years before he was obliged to leave The Custom Shop and becoming a full-fledged, full-time restaurateur.

Today Mortimer's is more successful, in its own way, than "21," America's oldest and most famous celebrity restaurant. "21" is now quite commercial—a tourist's stop for those who can afford it—a miniscule Waldorf-Astoria—but still a place in which to see and be seen. Mortimer's is quite personal, more selective, more intimate, and therein lies the difference.

It frequently happens that spectacularly successful restaurants come to a spectacularly crashing end, but Mortimer's has grown even stronger as it's gotten older. But let's begin at the beginning.

Glenn Bernbaum grew up on fashionable Delancey Place in downtown Philadelphia, and despite a down-to-earth level-headedness that one would expect from an exceptionally bright man, Glenn was fortunate in having been born a snob. This quality eventually served him well as a restaurateur.

Glenn's father was a senior executive and major stockholder in National Department Stores. Between the income from that business and his mother's inherited wealth, the Bernbaums lived in Main Line splendor—a handsome, beautifully maintained town house, a staff of servants, chauffeured limousines, country clubs, and all the rest.

Bernbaum received his B.A. degree from the University of Pennsylvania, and served in the U.S. Army during World War II, ending his military career as a captain in the psychological warfare division. His initial business experience was at Lousol's, a large ladies' high-fashion specialty store in Philadelphia owned by his family. The business was sold to Franklin Simon after the death of Glenn's father. Bernbaum was taken on at Franklin Simon as sales promotion manager and ready-to-wear merchandise manager, and subsequently promoted to general merchandise manager. After five years at Franklin Simon, he moved over to Korvette's, where he held the position of general merchandise manager for soft goods.

In those days, Eugene Ferkauf, the founder of Korvette's, was feeling his oats because of the enormous initial success his chain of stores was enjoying as a result of its deep discounting policy. However, Ferkauf had no background as a retailer, and no really strong knowledge of merchandising. He didn't realize that without strong inventory controls, he would soon be losing money. In a dispute with Loeb, Rhoades (Korvette's Wall Street underwriter) over the installation of point-of-sale recording equipment, Bernbaum resigned.

I picked Glenn up on the rebound for less than half what he had been accustomed to earning. Except for having an impossible temper, Bernbaum turned out to be exactly what The Custom Shop needed. He was the first truly professional merchant in my company (I certainly wasn't), and his earnings were quickly readjusted. Up till then, Custom Shop had been successful because of my basic concept of a no-frills/direct-to-the-consumer approach, with a service that was unique at my low prices. Bernbaum brought in a much-needed professionalism. He understood turnover, markup, and inventory control. We complemented each other, and The Custom Shop continued to prosper.

Glenn never married. He bought himself a handsome town house on East Fifty-second Street, and hired Parish-Hadley, decorators to the cognoscenti, as a consultant. He furnished his home with oil paintings and other *objets d'art*, most of which have quadrupled in value. He pursued two hobbies relentlessly: reading and cooking. He himself was a first-rate cook, and he also employed a gourmet cook, a Polish woman named Theresa Jankowski. Once a week, he invited me to lunch with him at his home. One day, my wife remarked offhandedly to Glenn about the absence of a desirable restaurant in our neighborhood, and said she would love to open one to fill that need. Glenn said he would like to open a restaurant too, with her, but not with me. Thus, an idea was born. One year later, when Glenn discovered that a restaurant named Tangerine, located at the corner of Lexington Avenue and Seventy-fifth Street, was in trouble and for sale, the idea was acted upon, but *without* Mimi.

Bernbaum decided he wanted to open a restaurant as a hobby, saying, "Why shouldn't I drink at my own bar instead of somebody else's bar?" I had all the hobbies and most of the money. Glenn was doing most of the work. It hardly seemed fair. So I had no objection to Bernbaum going ahead with plans for his restaurant *while he remained* as chief operating officer of The Custom Shop. It started out *only* as a hobby.

But let's ask the key question: Why should people eat at Mortimer's instead of where they had been eating? Here were several good reasons:

1. *Location.*   The site was convenient for all those affluent people living on the Upper East Side.
2. *Style.*   Glenn redid the place completely (for peanuts, I might add, but money never was a substitute for taste). It was attractive without being pretentious. It had a long bar, like a pub, bare brick walls, some good-sized

oil paintings, white tablecloths, cloth napkins, and very expensive flowers at each end of the bar.

3. *Quality.* Glenn is a really sophisticated cook who knows what good food should taste like, and he knows too how it should be served.

4. *Reputation.* He imported the saucier from London's famous Hotel Connaught, a fact that was quickly and very well publicized. And, of course, the new chef was helpful in bringing Glenn's cooking ideas to fruition.

5. *Efficiency.* Glenn is extremely bright, and a thoroughly disciplined, experienced businessman, a far cry from the usual restaurant owner. He runs Mortimer's like a business.

6. *Clientele.* Two of his closest friends are Bill Blass and Kenneth Jay Lane. Between them, they knew most of the world's beautiful people, and they were not averse to patronizing Mortimer's.

7. *Ambience.* Bernbaum, the born snob, practically made Mortimer's a club, treating the general public with indifference. In effect, Mortimer's became a private club with an exclusive membership but no dues.

8. *Price.* Add to all this the fact that the menu was a bargain. He set prices that were quite low. Bernbaum knew, having been born to affluence, that the rich (unlike the new rich) are quite careful with their money and appreciate value.

Mortimer's was swamped with business from day one. It won two stars from John Canaday, the never overly generous *New York Times* food critic of the day. Canaday wrote that he would have given the restaurant three stars if only the recorded music in the restaurant were played a few decibels lower.

Mortimer's initial success continued as Bernbaum ignored my advice in two ways. Prospective diners arrived, and the maître d' dutifully recorded their names in rotation as they came in. However, the tables were *not* given out in rotation. I pointed out to Glenn that some time in the future he might need all those people he was offending. He said he didn't want them and didn't care. Then I suggested that he have two seatings: one at seven and one at nine. He said, "Never! Let them walk. I want my restaurant to be like a club." And that's what it became—a meeting place for the beautiful people with lots of table-hopping. He accepted no reservations for fewer than five, but his friends and their friends always received preferential treatment.

Neither of us was prepared for the enormous and sudden success the restaurant achieved. This then presented another problem. Bernbaum could not very well run The Custom Shop's business (there were fifty-one branches at the time) and also operate a restaurant that required his presence from 8 A.M. to midnight, seven days a week. He considered selling the restaurant. One potential buyer came along, but when it became evident that he expected to pay for the restaurant "out of profits," Bernbaum demurred.

Finally, we agreed that Bernbaum would stay on at The Custom Shop part-time until his replacement could be found. Believe it or not, it took me three years to find that replacement.

Subsequently, with my encouragement, Glenn bought the building his restaurant was located in. That inadvertently turned out to be a bonanza because of the enormous increase in value of New York City real estate. When the adjoining store's lease was up, Glenn refused to renew it to the tenant and expanded his restaurant for the first time. He called the new room Also Mortimer's, and set it up for the late crowd. A pianist came in to play from eleven-thirty to two-thirty. Also Mortimer's doubled Glenn's income and expanded his select clientele even more.

He painted the entire five-story building a cream color— quite elegant. Then he cleaned up the Seventy-fifth Street side to open Café Mortimer, using outdoor tables and a canopy (newly allowed by the city's liberalized code) to encourage a Paris-like ambience. He commissioned a trompe l'oeil painting on the walls to add his creative touch outdoors.

Finally, when the lease ran out on the small Seventy-fifth Street store, he took that over too as an indoor Café Mortimer, serving a completely different menu and at the same time cashing in on the gourmet take-out food business that was flourishing in New York.

Glenn did make one mistake. Originally, the small Seventy-fifth Street store was occupied by an unprepossessing dress shop. When that lease ran out, Glenn took over the space and opened it as a gift shop in partnership with Kenneth Jay Lane, but it was unsuccessful.

The publicity Bernbaum and his restaurant have received in the past decade is staggering. He stopped using a publicist in the third year, but when you are a celebrity, publications seek you out. Mortimer's has had feature articles in *Town & Country, Vanity Fair, W, Women's Wear Daily*, and the *New York Times Magazine*, as well as frequent mention in New York's society columns. In addition, the restaurant is mentioned regularly by newspapers and magazines in London, Paris, and Rome with a full-page story in the international editon of the *Herald-Tribune* which is published in Paris. Last year, *New York* magazine ran a full-page photo on its cover with a major story on the restaurant, and *House and Garden* featured both the restaurant and Bernbaum's tastefully furnished apartment in a summer issue.

In recent years, Bernbaum added yet another dimension by producing private parties for his customers. He literally designs these functions (dinner parties up to 100, cocktail parties up to 250) with imagination and good taste, and each party gets its own special menu and special décor. The parties provide another source of income and an ever-expanding source of new and attractive customers.

The opening of Mortimer's had three advantages for me: (1) it brought The Custom Shop considerable publicity; (2) it provided me with four or five free lunches a year as Bernbaum's guest; and (3) it made room for Anthony Bergamo, a young, bright, overachieving lawyer, at The Custom Shop. As president, Bergamo took to the business like a duck to water. And I promoted myself to chairman of the board.

So Bernbaum is happy, Bergamo is happy, and I am happy. At this point, Glenn is missing only one thing: the chance to go on vacation for more than a week or two at a time. Unfortunately, his is the kind of business that demands constant attention. Without Glenn, there really is no Mortimer's.

I don't understand how Glenn can live with all that noise at lunch, at dinner, and then again at supper. But he says his clientele loves the noise. As for Bernbaum, the din is music to his ears.

# 12
■ □ ■

# STEVE ISRAEL
## Architectural Artifacts
## from Junk

America is described as the land of opportunity. But few of us, I think, realize just how many opportunities are out there for entrepreneurs. Sometimes it's a matter of recognizing what is before your eyes. Steve Israel was introduced to me as a businessman who had the vision to see profit in a most unlikely source: the architectural artifacts that were being discarded as junk by wrecking crews.

I found Israel to be not at all a businessman, although under the circumstances, he has done extraordinarily well. To me, he was Bohemian, a wide-ranging romantic.

Israel is the founder and chairman of the splendiferously titled Great American Salvage Company. His current headquarters is a 12,000-square-foot warehouse in Montpelier, Vermont. He also has a large store on New York's Cooper Square, plus branches in Jacksonville, Florida; New Haven, Connecticut; and Sag Harbor, Long Island.

STEVE ISRAEL, *founder and president, Great American Salvage Company*

At the age of thirty-seven, Israel is an overpowering physical presence: six feet four, 220 pounds, with a massive black beard, and a headful of superb black hair. He moved around so much at the beginning of his career that one gets dizzy trying to follow it.

After college (University of Bridgeport, B.A. in literature), Steve taught high school for two years in Stamford, Connecticut, and New York City. He had always been a city boy, but soon found public-school teaching impossible. He moved to Woodstock, New York, a well-known artists' colony in the forties, where a friend hired him as a carpenter —a kooky switch, it would appear, but Israel was actually quite capable with his hands.

During his spare time, in the ensuing five years, Steve built himself a small house in Woodstock—and when it was finished realized that he couldn't afford to live there. His sparse income wouldn't cover the expenses and taxes. He sold the house for $65,000 cash, and for the first time in his life had money in the bank. So off he went to the Bahamas. Obviously, this was not a man who lived for tomorrow.

Although he knew nothing about sailing, he decided to buy a boat and sail around the world. Then, faced with reality, he selected a more sober dream, to own a farm. He bought a small farm in Vermont with fifty cows, a few chickens, fifteen pigs, four horses, and two dilapidated buildings. Having fifty cows was like having fifty children. Steve did everything necessary to run his farm, beginning at four-thirty every morning, after which he went out to work as a carpenter, because he needed a regular income.

It was at this point that Steve's real aptitude came to light, and it turned out to be the beginning of his business. He was more than a carpenter; he had become a woodworker, and that gave him enormous respect for the workmanship that went into architecture. His random finds of architectural artifacts turned into a growing collection, and he began to store his *"objets d'art"*—odd pieces that were being thrown away as junk when old buildings were demolished. In the back of his mind, he thought these oddities would one day be valuable, and as it turned out, his hunch was right. He collected cornices, brackets, mantels, solid wooden doors (oak and mahogany), rooms of paneling, moldings, gargoyles, etc.

Israel had started his farming venture in 1976. By 1978, he realized he wasn't making any money. Then one day that spring, his bull got loose and in a frenzy of sexual frustration smashed half of his artifacts. Steve decided to sell the bull and the rest of his livestock and go about collecting architectural objects full-time. He and a friend, Steve Tillotson, a small home-building contractor, went into business together.

For Steve, as for most other entrepreneurs, the road to success had many ups and downs.

The business started officially when the partners rented a one-room storefront in Woodstock, Vermont, for the two-week period prior to Christmas. They placed small ads in the local paper and sent out a mailing to restaurants and businesses: "Presenting a collection of architectural antiques for two weeks only." They sold $3,500 worth of merchandise and made several valuable contacts. Their first big sale took place when they located a customer who wanted a quantity of stained glass for a restaurant. Steve knew about a large collection in Boston, drove there, invested all the profits from the Woodstock sale, and trucked it back. They sold half of the glass to the restaurant man at twice their cost.

At this point, Israel's partner opted for the security of a salaried job because he needed money every week to support his family. So Steve was back on his own. He next rented a one-room storefront in Montpelier. He selected the name Great American Salvage Company simply because he liked the sound. That move, however, turned out to be a bust. The store was on the second floor, and he sold next to nothing. He moved his inventory into an empty garage, bought a dip tank for chemically stripping wood, and the Great American Salvage Company used the revenue generated by that hand-to-mouth business as a way of staying afloat. He advertised his dipping business, and customers who came in to have furniture stripped occasionally bought his artifacts. As the artifact sales increased, Israel hired Tillotson on a part-time basis to run the dipping business, freeing Steve to seek out additional treasures.

In 1980, a handsome post-and-beam warehouse became available on Main Street in Montpelier at $1,000 a month. Steve moved his entire inventory and dipping business there, and it has remained his home office.

Great American Salvage did only $250,000 worth of business between 1980 and 1983. Not a large volume, but it was a living. Everything was reinvested for inventory, equipment, a larger pickup truck, etc. At this point, our hero's business was paying him a salary of about $250 a week. Tillotson, now a full-time employee, was being paid $250 a week, and a part-time saleswoman earned $6 an hour. In addition, there was a part-time carpenter who earned $4 an hour, and a rent-exchange agreement with a young artist who also received nominal pay for the stained-glass restoration work he did for the company.

Then Al Corwin, a long-time friend of Israel and his family, became interested in Steve's vision of a burgeoning market for the artifacts. Incredibly (to me), Corwin was able to put together a small group of architectural-artifact fans who put up a total of *$250,000 for 25 percent* of a business that was paying the proprietor a salary of *only $250 a week*. The money was raised partly on the basis of the large inventory that had been accumulating over the years, partly because of the growth potential of the business, and partly out of a shared interest, similar to the interest one might have for modern paintings.

One of Israel's marketing efforts had been a direct-mail letter to interior designers, architects, and department-store display directors. This brought Bloomingdale's Colin Birch to Steve's door, and a resulting contract with Bloomingdale's in New York City gave investors the courage to go ahead. Bloomingdale's put Steve and the Great American Salvage Company on the map in a big way.

Bloomingdale's was planning one of its storewide annual promotions, this time celebrating "Americana." Steve received a contract for $50,000 to design, build, and install a tract of Americana storefronts on Bloomingdale's sixth floor.

Israel engaged a team of fifteen carpenters and within three weeks had erected 400 linear feet of storefront in his Vermont warehouse. It was all built from the salvage of his own inventory. Unfortunately, it was a labor-intensive project, and Steve miscalculated that aspect when he agreed to the $50,000 fee. Although he made no money on the deal, he gained considerable prestige. Bloomingdale's was so pleased with the results of the promotion that they offered Steve another contract in Texas. But Steve said no to that —he had had enough.

Anyway, in 1983 Great American Salvage located a two-story store in New York City on historic Cooper Square, with 16,000 square feet of space. They opened this giant store with part of the $250,000 generated by the sale of their stock.

Unfortunately, the new store in New York was slow in getting off the ground, and actually lost money in its first year. However, the location generated so much publicity he was able to expand again, this time through a licensing agreement with two groups, one in Jacksonville, and the other in New Haven.

Great American Salvage broadened its market by giving more people access to the inventory. This was accomplished with a computerized listing of inventory accompanied by videocassettes and photographs for all three branches. The system permitted all future inventory to be graphically displayed on computer terminals in each store.

However, because 1984 was not a good year, Great American Salvage found it necessary to raise additional capital. This time an offering of 9 percent debenture bonds raised $175,000.

The nationwide interest in antiques would indicate that after a varied and shaky start, the Great American Salvage Company is on its way. The story of Israel's success is perhaps a little premature. He has yet to prove that he can make big money, but I would think that many of my readers would be reasonably happy to own a business that returns a $100,000 annual profit.

The one negative feeling I had about Steve's business was the difficulty he would have in finding additional artifacts. But he tells me that he is being offered more material than he can ever dispose of. That is one of the reasons for the licensing agreements, which he sees as the real future of the Great American Salvage Company. That remains to be seen, but meanwhile what a happy ending for a landlubber who wanted to sail around the world alone!

MIKE WEATHERLY, *president and CEO, The Forschner Group*

# 13

■ □ ■

# MIKE WEATHERLY
## Carving Out a Fortune
## with the Swiss Army Knife

Mike Weatherly is a handsome, young-looking fifty-four.
His wife, Ellis, is a most attractive blonde, an A skier,
a high-B tennis player, a sublime cook, and a lively hostess.
She brought three children to this, her second marriage. It
was Mike's third marriage, and he brought four children—
not exactly one-upmanship, because they have merged, and
very successfully.

Weatherly received his B.A. degree with honors in political science at Princeton. He was a popular campus figure
as an undergraduate, and his tennis, boating club, and ROTC
contacts from Princeton have served him well in business.
He is personable enough to have become a diplomat, but as
it turned out, he undoubtedly did better in business. In all
candor, his business career has been mildly irregular, even
bumpy, but not without a certain fascination.

As a result of ROTC, Mike served two years as a lieutenant in the Army in Germany. Again, thanks to ROTC, he took an M.B.A. at the government's expense from the Harvard Business School in 1958. In earning this credential, he cultivated still more contacts, which he would use to his advantage, along with a surplus of self-confidence and charm.

In those days, M.B.A.'s had four popular career choices: Wall Street, marketing, retailing, or advertising. Weatherly selected advertising at the prestigious firm of Dancer, Fitzgerald & Sample. He was assigned to the Procter & Gamble account as assistant account executive. Procter & Gamble, the world's largest and most progressive company making and marketing consumer products, has probably "graduated" more top-level marketing executives than Harvard.

It's interesting to take a look back at the salaries: Weatherly started at $5,500 a year. Today's M.B.A. expects to get between $35,000 and $80,000. More specifically, Mike's stepson Chris with a B.S. in business from Wharton, started at Citibank's investment banking division at the age of twenty-three for $31,000. How times have changed!

At Procter & Gamble, Mike soon discovered he was not even a technician. The individual product manager, who writes the marketing strategy, was responsible for the individual product. Actually, however, marketing strategy was determined by the top brass; the function of the product manager seemed to be endless memos that were refinements on both the figures and the marketing strategy conceived upstairs. Key questions like what is the product objective, what is the advertising objective, to whom do we aim our message, to which socioeconomic scales, how and when do we first test the advertising, etc., were not left to product managers to handle on their own.

As a result, to his great surprise, Weatherly discovered he was bored with Madison Avenue and the unchallenging role to which he had been assigned. He had the itch to get into a business of his own. Meanwhile, he had married and was fortunate to have access to his wife's money for whatever financing a modest new venture might need. (An interesting phenomenon was occurring at the time. Rich boys were beginning to marry poor girls, and rich girls were beginning to marry poor boys—instead of living together as they do now. And the M.B.A.'s, being better positioned than other poor boys, were indeed marrying money. And that's what happened to Mike.)

Weatherly's career as an entrepreneur started at a cocktail party in 1960, when he met a handsome, white-haired professor of philosophy named John W. Blyth, dean of Hamilton College in upstate New York. Mike was twenty-eight. Professor Blyth was pioneering a new method of learning by creating training courses using programmed learning techniques in booklet form. Mike was fascinated.

Blyth had recently left academia to join the consulting group of John Diebold, the computer wizard. Blyth's "students" were businessmen and salesmen. For example, pharmaceutical companies like Pfizer, Johnson & Johnson, and Warner-Lambert had large sales staffs calling on doctors to introduce new medications. That sales force went to training classes once or twice a week for up to eighteen months. In contrast, the average time spent talking to doctors during a sales call was only three minutes. The programmed instruction course that Dr. Blyth custom-tailored would zero in on those three minutes, condensing the year and a half of training into three hours. The possibilities for the future of such a business were intriguing to Mike, and he said so to Dr. Blyth.

They went into business together, calling their new business Argyle Publishing Inc. In addition to custom-tailored training programs for individual companies, they developed a series of generic programs that almost any company could use with its sales force. These were offered by direct mail to training directors. Mike put up all the capital: $15,000 —$3,000 to buy stock in the new corporation, and $12,000 as a loan. With that $15,000, they set up an office and hired a secretary. Profits were to be divided seventy-thirty, 70 percent to Mike, 30 percent to Blyth. Salaries were $30,000 for Blyth, $25,000 for Weatherly.

It seemed to me as Mike related the start-up that there was insufficient reason to go into this business. Dr. Blyth was offering nothing that was not already being offered by Xerox, IBM, and others. Even Diebold was offering similar courses, and as I heard it, the partners seemed to have no competitive advantage. But let's see what happened.

The business was never really profitable, because the product was underpriced. An average course was $10.95, with discounts for 50, 100, and 250 "students." But there was nothing to stop a company from buying twenty-five programs and copying additional pages as needed. Then Argyle made the mistake of increasing overhead by hiring staff writers instead of using free-lance writers. Weatherly discovered, too, that going into partnership with Dr. Blyth was like going into partnership with another Hemingway. Blyth was a gifted business writer, but treated every piece of training literature as a treatise, which meant that deadlines came and went while he continued to agonize over every word.

In 1965, at the end of their fourth year, annual sales volume had reached only $264,000. The business, meanwhile, had been supported by infusions of cash from Weatherly's wife. And unfortunately, Mike's first marriage was struggling as much as his business.

It is obvious that sales were not sufficient to continue paying two high salaries. It had survived only because (so it seemed at the time) good money was being thrown after bad. All told, Mike's wife put in about $80,000, and there was no way Weatherly could repay it. To the rescue came Louis Marx, Jr., Mike's long-time friend, a tennis buddy from Princeton, son and heir of Louis Marx the toy king. Marx offered to buy 40 percent of the company for $80,000, and Mike jumped at the chance.

Argyle's track record was poor, yet a potential still seemed to exist, especially for one not intimately acquainted with its problems. Dan Lufkin, cofounding partner of the investment banking firm of Donaldson, Lufkin & Jenrette, believed that the business had "sizzle" and a public offering would be well received. As it turned out, Lufkin was right, meaning that Louis Marx's original saving gesture had been shrewd as well as friendly.

Argyle Publishing made a public offering in 1967. Because it was less than $300,000, it was not required to be submitted to the Securities and Exchange Commission. No underwriter was used, not even a financial printer. Mike called up his Wall Street contacts and quickly sold 75,000 shares at $4 a share. He later said he could have sold 750,000 shares because of Blyth's distinguished credentials. Outside investors now owned 16 percent of Argyle Publishing. Marx and Lufkin sold 16 percent of nothing, really, for $300,000.

*However*, their prospectus just happened to land on the desk of John W. Kluge. Kluge was in the news in 1986 when he sold the cellular telephone division of his Metromedia for $1.4 billion and, prior to that, when he sold some of his television stations for some $3 billion.

By this time, there had been a further development in the Blyth teaching program. In addition to the printed materials, audio tapes and video programs had been developed, thus permitting instructions and reinforcement to come directly from the instructor.

Kluge phoned Mike, and believe it or not, two interviews

later, Kluge said, "I want to buy your company." Mike said the business was for sale but it had to bring more than the $4 a share for which they had just gone public. As there were 460,000 shares, a $5-per-share price would come to $2.3 million. Mike said, "Mr. Kluge, the sales volume is two hundred sixty-four thousand dollars, and we lost fifty thousand dollars last year." But Kluge, who was both smart and stupendously successful, believed that Mike and Blyth lacked the know-how to market their great idea properly. So he said, "That doesn't worry me, Mr. Weatherly, I'll buy your company." And he did.

Mike's friend Louis Marx made a $1 million profit from his $80,000 investment, after which he said, "Never has so much been paid for so little."

John Kluge retained both Blyth and Mike as part of the deal. Mike suggested moving Argyle Publishing to La Jolla, California (where he could play tennis year-round). Kluge said no. But Weatherly moved his home to La Jolla anyway, leaving Blyth to spend his eighteen-hour days writing the various instructional programs that were the cornerstone of the business. Mike was fired as soon as Kluge realized that he wasn't "minding the store."

However, this time Kluge's judgment turned out to be wrong. Even after he fired Mike, he couldn't make the business work, and he closed it two years later. Kluge had earned the right to be wrong, and this was yet another example of the "easy come, easy go" syndrome. For Mike, it was perfectly all right. He and his second wife were enjoying their new life in La Jolla; where life revolved around their swimming pool and their tennis court.

It was 1970 and real estate was hot in California. So, and maybe for the first time in his business career, Weatherly put his nose to the grindstone by earning himself a real-estate broker's license. "It was kind of like being back in school again," he said.

And it was also the era of modular housing. Mike, along with two associates, both real-estate salesmen, and an architect, developed a unique concept for a mini housing development. They could build a complete modular (prefabricated) apartment of only 386 square feet. That idea, once again, was the result of a conversation Mike had with a man at a cocktail party.

Weatherly formed a new company called Growth Area Associates with $500,000. Louis Marx, Jr., put in $200,000 ($20,000 in equity and $180,000 as a loan); $200,000 came from other Argyle "alumni"; and the final $100,000 came from Mike.

So the business was started. The four partners bought a piece of land, and the first building was built. The apartments were rented furnished, by the month, and turned out to be quite profitable. The second unit was in the planning stage.

One morning, Weatherly was sitting by his pool contemplating his good life when Marx telephoned from New York. "Mike, I've got the perfect thing for Growth Area Associates. I just bought 2.5 million acres of soft pine in Honduras for $3 million. I want you to fly down to Honduras and check it all out—the territory, the sawmills, the dredging, and the logging equipment." Then Marx insisted, "I want you to run the new company." And indeed, this seemed to be a really enormous opportunity. Mike sold Growth Area Associates for a modest profit to the two real-estate brokers who, sadly, did not fully appreciate Mike's concept of low rents. In the end, the venture failed. Fortunately, all of Weatherly's original investors did get their money back.

The new lumber venture was incorporated in 1972 and called Wincom (formed from "winning" and "combination"). They decided to combine the pine business with Marx's oil holdings, Viking Oil. Once again, they made a public offering. Someone else was put in charge of the lumber business, and Mike was sent to the Far East to buy additional oil leases to supplement the leases Viking was already holding.

Mike became a 25 percent shareholder in Viking Oil, by investing $150,000 in the new venture. And after the company went public, Mike's 25 percent was valued (on paper) at $18 million. I have yet to learn who the people are who invest their hard-earned money so carelessly, and who are the conscienceless stockbrokers who offer this meaningless paper to a gullible public.

Legally, Marx and Mike could have sold their stock, and Weatherly suggested that they do just that, but Marx said they must wait, for appearance's sake at least, until the company was more mature.

In 1973, happenstance took over again, this time in Honduras. The government squeezed them out. "We lost our shirts." Export duties were tripled overnight, making it impossible to export their lumber because it was no longer competitive. Colonel Oswaldo López, the president of Honduras, offered to buy the company for 30 cents on the dollar in long-term Honduran bonds. Mike said, "Why don't you throw in some bananas?" The colonel patted his gun and said, "Gringo, no joke."

They finally settled for 30 cents on the dollar in cash. Unfortunately, the bad luck didn't stop there. They drilled dry wells in the Maldive Islands, in China, and in Taiwan. In Canada, their existing wells went dry. They put in additional capital as needed to cover the near-ruinous losses that were taking place. Mike went from $18 million in net worth on paper to $2 million in debt. Woeful is the life of the speculator.

This brings our story up to 1974. Mike moved back east to Fairfield, Connecticut, which is where I met him for the first time. One day, he received a phone call from Dick

Prentiss, Jr., another one of his tennis-playing friends from Princeton, and that call marked the beginning of Mike's current business—the business that is the real reason I've included Weatherly as a model entrepreneur.

"I think you and Louis might be interested in buying my father's knife business, the Forschner Company. He is now seventy-five and getting ready to retire." The business had sales of $4 million, $3 million in cutlery and $1 million in the Swiss Army knife. Forschner's net profit was $300,000, and Prentiss wanted a $2 million certified check for Forschner's (about seven times earnings) and would include receivables, inventory, good will, everything.

Mike needed a job, but he didn't want *just* a job; he wanted, once again, to have his own company. Marx's accountants analyzed the books and confirmed Prentiss's figures.

There is usually a subliminal reason for selling a business. It is true that Mr. Prentiss was aging, but it was also true that the value of the dollar had fallen about 27 percent in one year, meaning the cost of landing Forschner's merchandise would increase in proportion. The question then was, would it still be competitive?

So once again Mike went to Marx, saying, "This is a great business; let's do it." Marx wasn't really interested, but had some guilt feelings for having dragged Mike away from his real-estate operation. Marx was finally persuaded when Mike pointed out that they could borrow $1 million on Forschner's inventory and receivables. They borrowed $1 million at 4 percent over prime, an annual interest of 16 percent, much too high for a legitimate enterprise. Marx put up $250,000 to buy stock in the company and $750,000 as a loan. They made a handshake deal in which Mike was promised 20 percent of the business as a finder's fee in the event the company was ever sold. His salary arrangement was left open and would depend upon how the venture fared.

The $300,000 profit was being made after a $75,000 salary had been paid to Prentiss Sr. Weatherly set that salary for himself also. Prentiss Sr. stayed on for six months, taking Mike to Switzerland, introducing him to the source of the merchandise, and showing him how the business had been run. At the end of six months, Weatherly was left on his own.

In 1974, the year before Mike bought the business, Swiss Army knife sales were $1 million. In 1986, Swiss Army knife sales were $20 million. During this same period, Forschner's cutlery sales increased from $3 million to $10 million. But the spectacular increase in the knife business and the tiny twist that made it happen are what make the whole story worth reading.

Forschner had thirteen distributors and in addition about forty accounts to whom it sold directly. The distributors had been using the Swiss Army knife as a loss leader to induce customers to buy their cutlery. That is, except for one distributor—he sold more of the Swiss Army knives than all the others put together. Why? Simply because he had created a small display case to be mounted on the counter right next to the cash register. It was large enough to display the complete line of Army knives. And the case was so constructed that the knives could not be removed, meaning that the full line was always on display, at precisely the place customers were paying for their purchases.

Mike decided to give up all the distributors, except for the one. By the remotest coincidence, his prize-winning distributor turned out to be a poor businessman and was already in debt to Forschner. Mike acquired his distributorship and in turn hired the distributor as a salesman.

The salesman went to work and quite quickly sold the display cases to mass merchandisers: Herman's, Caldor, Wal-Mart, Best Products, Service Merchandise, et al. Mike's staff then followed up each installation with monthly phone calls to make sure the stores filled in their inventories. All told, there were forty-two different knives.

Today there are now some 12,000 of these display cases around the country, and it is quite easy to understand why the volume jumped from $1 million to $20 million in twelve years. And because they were now distributing the merchandise directly, they eliminated the distributor's profit, meaning the company was working with an even higher gross margin.

There was one further reason for their increased sales. A new salesman with a different background suggested that the company enter the specialty advertising field: small Swiss Army knives that corporations could give to clients and employees; knives that would also carry the corporate logo on the handle or cover. That end of the business turned out to be surprisingly successful and today accounts for a big 35 percent of their total sales. But of course when one is in business, chance is bound to play an important role, just because the business exists. Sometimes it is good; sometimes it is bad.

Unfortunately, there is frequently a fly in the ointment. Marx couldn't let well enough alone. He bought yet another business. Here is a brief summary of the "basket business." An old friend suggested that Marx buy Skalny Baskets, a most reputable company that imported baskets (all kinds), mainly from Poland. Polish willow is exceptional in quality and appearance. Skalny sold the business because China was moving into the basket business in a big way, and it would be hard for the Polish product to compete. Neither Marx nor his friend was aware of this, another case of that damaging 5 percent that you don't learn about until it is too late.

The friend had a well-established reputation in the corporate world, but he had never run a small business. After China entered the market, business got tougher for Skalny. So Marx asked Mike to take over the management of that company too. For a short time, Mike was able to turn the business around. He opened up fourteen retail stores in Connecticut called Baskets and Blades. Their first shop was opened in a small discount shopping center in Norwalk, Connecticut. It was relatively successful. At least it was profitable. Then they quickly opened thirteen more. The new stores were losing money, and a decision was made to close the shops. Buying out the leases was expensive for the company, and ultimately Forschner's liquidated the basket business with a $2.5 million loss. Obviously, it was a mistake to open so many stores so fast. And that happened because neither Weatherly nor Marx had any prior experience as retailers. But they were smart to get out. (There is an established business axiom, "The first loss is usually the smallest loss—take it and run.")

When Marx put Forschner's into the basket business in 1979, he was obliged to lend them an additional $1.5 million, and his debt position in the company rose to $2.8 million. So once again Mike and Marx made a public offering—in 1983, of $5 million. And once again they found buyers and Marx got his money back.

So that Mike could have an ownership position in the company he was running, Louis loaned Mike $1 million to buy 20 percent of the company, 333,333 shares.

At this writing, it would seem Mike has it made: a very comfortable living out of a company in which he has a strong financial position, with a product that seems to have universal appeal. Happenstance played a strong role in Weatherly's string of unfailing successes, but it was his endless charm and optimistic outlook that made it all possible.

If at first you don't succeed, try, try again.

# 14

· □ ·

# GENE BALLIN
## A True Entrepreneur
## Invents His Own
## Opportunities

Unlike Mike Weatherly, for whom unforeseen events conspired almost magically to ensure success in his various business ventures, unforeseen events conspired to spoil many of Gene Ballin's entrepreneurial efforts. Gene Ballin is innately gifted—a real-life inventor—but he has seen several promising businesses compromised by happenstance. Yet he has persisted, demonstrating an exceptional if not quixotic talent for picking himself up, shaking himself off, and starting all over again. It's impossible to overrate such a quality in the fickle world of free enterprise.

Ballin carries two business cards, one identifying him as president of Tyz-All Plastics; the other as "Creative Engineer." The image projected by his cards does not do him justice: inexpensive stock, thermographic printing, and a modernistic layout, indicating, to my eye at least, a taste level in graphics that, happily, was not evidenced in his

GENE BALLIN, *president and CEO, Tyz-All Plastics, Inc.*

person. He is a distinguished-looking man with graying hair and friendly blue-gray eyes. He was born in 1919 and looks ten years younger than his present sixty-nine.

Ballin entered City College as an engineering student, but his faculty adviser suggested that he switch to a liberal-arts major, explaining that anti-Semitism (those were different times) would make it virtually impossible for him to land a job as an engineer. He switched, but was not altogether happy with the liberal-arts education he was getting. So when a chance came to apply for a Cooper Union scholarship in architecture, he took it. At sixteen, he became the youngest student ever to have received a Cooper Union scholarship. Demonstrating the true entrepreneur's penchant for obsessive application, he went to City College by day and Cooper Union at night.

Meanwhile, a buxom and aggressive eighteen-year old girl had moved into the apartment house where his family lived. She had encountered Gene several times in the hallway when one day, suddenly, she kissed him sensuously on the mouth. That kiss, he recalls today, sparked a motivation that channeled his energy into a desire to make money. Until then, he had been devoted to study for study's sake.

Now he needed money to take the girl out, at least for an ice-cream soda. There was no money to be had at home. Out of desperation, he said to himself, "I'll invent something." And he did—a combination comb and brush. In a most unusual procedure, he achieved an audience with the president of Venida, a subsidiary of Woolworth dealing in products for the hair. Gene showed a model that he had made with his own hands out of a cream-cheese box, using toothpicks as bristles. He sold the patent to Venida for $2,500 plus a half-cent royalty on every unit manufactured. No units were ever made, but still, it was quite an achievement for a seventeen-year-old.

Ballin developed a strong interest in aeronautical engineering, so after graduation, at the tail end of the Depression, he spent three months visiting aviation plants in the East. In those days, one had to list religion on employment applications. In two cases, his application was torn up while he watched; so there was no mistaking the truth that anti-Semitism was very much the factor his adviser had warned him about.

Undaunted, Ballin said, "If that's the game, I'll change my name to Ronald Vinson and list myself as Christian." He landed a job immediately with an aeronautical subcontractor, and subsequently with the New York Ordnance District as an ordnance inspector. He remained there until he was called to duty as an infantry officer, a result of prior ROTC training.

During his service in the Army, Gene submitted three inventions: (1) a bomb sight; (2) a tank transmission; and (3) an antitank gun and sight. They were accepted by the Army and patented. While he received no payment for these inventions, these patented inventions did result in an immediate promotion and a transfer from Infantry to Ordnance.

I said, "Gene, with your lack of background, how could you come up with three such highly technical inventions?" And Gene said, "I've been inventing things since childhood; I *am* an inventor—a compulsive searcher for new ways to do things, anything."

Ballin was in the Army from 1942 to 1946. Somewhere along the line, he decided that plastics were the wave of the future. He took a correspondence course from the U.S. Armed Forces Institute, intending to go into the plastics business for himself after the war. However, when he finally arrived home, he was shocked to learn that his wife had spent the money he had been sending her from overseas, erasing the modest bank account he had been depending on for setting up his own business. And this despite the fact that her father was a well-to-do developer and an owner of considerable real estate.

Ballin found a job at $75 a week as an assistant to a developer who was building homes in Atlantic Beach, a seaside resort in the Rockaways, Nassau County, but still part of the Greater New York metropolitan area. He learned fast and five months later met a man who agreed to let Gene design *and* build a private home on the man's own site. The client would save about 20 percent, and Gene would have his first opportunity as an entrepreneur. He charged the developer a bargain-basement fee of $3,000 for designing and overseeing the construction; it was 1946 and he was twenty-six. For the next three years, Ballin designed and built custom-made homes for clients who came to him through recommendations.

In 1949, he found a large parcel of land in East Rockaway (sixty-seven home sites) that was priced far below the market; "sale priced," actually, because it had a much-too-high water table. With his engineering know-how, Gene was sure he could resolve the water problem, a problem caused by a layer of clay under the surface that stopped the water from draining. He needed $1,000 to put down as a binder for the land plus $13,000 to start construction of a model home. Alas, Gene's wife had been terribly extravagant again, so that at the end of three years of building all those homes, Gene's entire capital consisted of only $1,000.

Ballin's father-in-law refused to lend him the money he needed. But Gene kept badgering him, and in a weak moment, the father-in-law finally gave in with, "All right, already, you can have it." The money was paid back in full in about four months from the deposits Gene received from the new buyers.

Finally, Gene could open his own business. He designed a model home for the project that went on to win a prize as the best ranch house of its class in the entire country for that year. He sold all sixty-seven homes in one day—it was the heart of the postwar building boom (happenstance).

He solved the water problem at the site by bringing in cranes to dig a series of large holes. The holes were filled with gravel through which the trapped water could drain. The cranes cost much more than the $13,000 he had originally borrowed. But clever Gene waited until he had sold all the houses, collected the deposits, and then brought in the cranes. Gene was thirty when he effected this coup.

The project was most profitable, and Ballin was in clover. In 1950, he started his second development, this time in Hewlett Harbor, an area close by. He bought a tract of land large enough to build fifty homes on one-acre plots. His model home was priced at $29,500, and once again all fifty homes were sold quickly—this time within a week.

Now, unfortunately, fate intervened in the form of the Korean War. Within two weeks of the outbreak of that conflict, prices for concrete, lumber, electrical wiring, etc., in fact, everything but appliances (which had already been contracted for) went up enormously—25 percent, and in some cases even more. There was no longer any way that Gene could build those homes for $29,500. Yet legally he was committed. Disaster!

Ballin called his buyers together and explained what had happened to prices as a result of the war. Therefore, he needed $6,000 more per house. He would contribute $3,500 per house from his personal funds if they agreed to pay an additional $2,500. If they did not agree, he would declare bankruptcy, in which case they would have legal fees but no homes. (The Act of War clause, which would have resolved his problem, was not in common use for building contracts.) I don't really understand *why* Gene went that route. If I had been in his place, I would have suggested completing the contract on a time-and-material basis, not to exceed X dollars. In any case, it took Gene a long time to pay off the debts resulting from a misfortune that neither he nor anyone else could have foreseen. Fact: When you own your own business, unpredictable problems frequently lie in wait.

Ballin paid no attention to that well-worn piece of kitchen philosophy, "Once bitten, twice shy." Three years later, he joined up with two other men to build 460 homes in Oceanside, once again in the same general area. That project, happily, was very successful and left him with enough capital to continue building homes, without partners. Ballin eventually became one of the area's biggest developers. In 1966, he bought thirty-six acres in Queens for $4 million. It was the first time he had moved out of Nassau County. On the day he broke ground for his model home, a squad car came by. The policeman introduced himself and said, "The lieutenant asked me to see you; it's going to cost you fifty dollars a house." Gene asked, "What for?" and the policeman said, "Every builder pays." Gene understood. But that was only the beginning. The policeman was followed by the building inspector, the plumbing inspector, the electrical inspector, the fire inspector, and by each of the union business agents. In spite of all these totally unexpected payoffs, Gene sold 200 homes, profitably, out of the planned 460. Within three months, 196 of those 200 houses were under construction.

At this point, the plumbers went on strike. The other unions quickly followed.

Gene was worth $3 million on paper. Construction was stopped for the full year that the strike lasted. His $3 million in paper profits remained, but all his cash had gone for interest on mortgages, building loans, taxes, payroll, security, etc. This time, Gene decided he was no longer going to be a developer.

Over the years, Ballin had accumulated several patents for the packaging industry, and his wife suggested that he try to market them. It took only three weeks for him to sell one patent to Borden. It was a container that automatically dispensed milk to feed infants in hospitals. Unfortunately, two years later Borden went out of the milk business and turned the patent back to Gene.

In 1975, Gene developed a plastic tie for use in packaging, which, incidentally, led him to his present business. The original tie was used most specifically for closing plastic garbage bags, yet another new industry. The "tie" business did very nicely due to a huge contract with Union Carbide. Unfortunately, that income dried up when Union Carbide created and manufactured a bag that required no tie.

But for Gene, as well as for the rest of us, the world keeps turning. The oil crisis and the need to conserve energy provided a new opening for Gene's ingenuity. In 1978, Scovill, a major manufacturer of metal button snaps, zippers, and the like, asked Ballin to design an *interior* plastic storm window. But as it happened, Scovill experienced cash-flow difficulties just at the moment that Gene's Remarkable Interior Storm Window was ready for production.

Gene bought the patent back from Scovill and went into business with a partner who was to be in charge of production. He marketed the window under a private label, introducing it at the Hardware Show in Chicago in 1978 with the claim that these "Remarkable Plastic Sheet Windows" could save homeowners up to 55 percent on their heating bills. Manufacturers' representatives took on the product, and buyers from the mass merchandisers placed orders. In all, Ballin sold 40,000 kits that first year, 360,000 the second year, and 700,000 the third year. He had applied for and received a $300,000 loan from the Small Business Administration, which he has since repaid.

Curiously enough, despite the fact that fuel oil became more plentiful and the price of oil dropped, more and more people became interested in the savings potential and the added comfort of these inexpensive windows. Yearly sales of this type of storm window keep increasing, but intense competition (and there's the rub) has lowered Gene's profit margin considerably.

Ballin has decided to sell his present business, saying, "I want to be alone. I want to go back to the beginning and live out my life as an inventor; that's when I was the happiest."

Ballin is not exactly a typical entrepreneur, and his experience points out only too clearly that starting your own business does not necessarily mean a happy ending. Ballin, in effect, has gone into business approximately ten times, each new real-estate development and invention being a business of its own. There is a difference, however, between a real-estate development, which is built to be sold, and starting a business like The Custom Shop or the Remarkable Interior Storm Window Company, which is intended to go on and on and on.

Despite all of Ballin's beginnings, he finally concluded that his métier was working for himself as an inventor, and he is left with sufficient funds to pursue that ephemeral career. The time factor it takes to conceive and develop an invention and its eventual successful production and marketing can seem like an eternity, but when it hits, it can really be big, producing the kind of income that dreams are made of.

JAMES MCMANUS, *founder and CEO, Marketing Corporation of America*

# 15
■ □ ■

## JAMES McMANUS
## A Money-making Smorgasbord of Marketing, Advertising, and Management Innovations

The only negative thing I can say about Jim McManus, founder of Marketing Corporation of America (MCA), is that he is not photogenic. He is a good-looking man, but his photographs just don't do him justice. Everything else does, however, including the handsome new office buildings he designed and built for his company headquarters on the banks of the Saugatuck River in Westport, Connecticut, and his attitude toward his colleagues, his employees, his family, his friends, and the town of Westport itself. (In the past six years, Jim has contributed about $1.5 million to support various nonprofit organizations in the town. No one else has ever come close to being that generous.) Although McManus is beholden to no one, he comports himself like

a man for whom "all men are created equal." And his mul-
titudinous activities as an entrepreneur are more than food
for thought—they are the making of a feast.

McManus founded MCA in 1971 as a proprietor. He is
now the chief executive officer and the majority stockholder
of twelve different companies within MCA. Each corporation operates profitably under its own president, and in 1986
this family of companies had revenues in excess of $400
million. Here then is a list of the twelve companies:

1. BFD Color Inserts—provides full-color, free-standing,
   co-op coupon inserts.*
2. Newspaper Co-op Couponing—the largest distributor
   of newspaper coupons in America, providing coupons
   at the lowest cost available.*
3. MCA Marketing Consulting—shows clients how to
   generate additional sales (and profits) from existing
   businesses.
4. MCA Market Research—provides clients with information on issues related to future marketing decisions, ideas for both new businesses and businesses
   already established.
5. MCA Sales Promotion—develops and executes creative promotion programs.
6. MCA Development Consulting—provides strategic
   planning to generate growth through new marketing
   strategies, new asset base configurations, new products and/or suggested acquisitions.
7. Ally Gargano/MCA Advertising—acquired in 1986, a
   full-service advertising agency that currently bills over
   $350 million with twenty-two clients. The agency is

*BFD Color Inserts and Newspaper Co-op Couponing divisions were both sold in
November 1986, but for purposes of illustration, I have included them in MCA's
story.

unique because it operates on a "seniors only" basis, staffed exclusively with highly experienced (no trainees) creative and marketing talent.

8. Business Express—the Delta Airline connection in the Northeast, created to meet the needs of corporate executives for connecting flights to major markets; currently the fastest-growing regional airline.

9. Westport Restaurants—administers Tanglewoods restaurants, a chain of medium-priced, tastefully decorated restaurants, serving good food, mostly in better-quality shopping centers.

10. Micro Education Corporation of America (MECA)—creates and markets innovative software for personal computers. The company began with the software version of that blockbuster book, Andrew Tobias's *Managing Your Money.*

11. MarketCorp Real Estate—provides a broad range of real estate investment and management services.

12. MarketCorp Venture Associates—venture-capital partnership formed to invest in consumer-oriented start-up and early-stage companies that are marketing-driven.

Now come the questions: How did Jim get where he is? How did this whole business start? What was the idea he had and where did he get the money?

To start at the beginning, McManus earned his M.B.A. in marketing at Northwestern University, and then was fortunate enough to start working for Procter & Gamble. He turned out to be yet another one of the marketing managers who came up through the ranks in the P&G marketing environment. He was there for eight years before leaving to join Ralph Glendinning (another P&G graduate), who had opened a promotional corporation in Westport. At the time our story begins, McManus was a senior executive at Glendinning, and had been there for seven years.

In 1970, he had the germ of a new idea that he felt certain could succeed. One night in October of that year, Jim said to his wife Nancy that, in pursuit of the new idea, he wanted to leave Glendinning and open his own business. With Nancy's blessing, Jim spent the next two months developing a business plan that he then presented to a friend in Minnesota, Curt Carlson. Carlson offered to invest $250,000 for a 50 percent interest in the company. Done!

So on February 1, 1971, McManus told Ralph he was resigning to start a similar business. He said that he would not take any Glendinning employees or solicit any Glendinning accounts for one year. However, he did want permission to make an offer to the four men that he, McManus, had attracted to Glendinning in the first place. They had become, so to speak, McManus's team, and having brought them to Glendinning, Jim felt he had the moral right to offer them employment. Obviously, he could have taken them without *any* discussion, but his need to do the right thing made that impossible. Included in the entrepreneur's risk—in this case Glendinning's—is the loss of valuable executives the entrepreneur may have trained. It is part of the price one must pay for taking the lion's share of the profit.

The four executives accepted McManus's offer on the spot, without even asking what their salaries would be. Jim said they would open for business in March.

Now—and this was interesting to me, for Jim's experience with Carlson was similar to my own experience with Seligson—McManus flew out to Minneapolis to formalize their contract. Jim learned then what my mother had taught me years and years ago: "There's many a slip 'twixt the cup and the lip." Fifteen minutes into the meeting, Carlson said,

"Jim, my lawyers tell me I must have fifty-one percent of the stock." It took McManus fifteen seconds to say he couldn't enter into an agreement unless he had 51 percent, meaning complete control. Jim found himself with no alternative way of financing his business, yet he wouldn't go ahead with Carlson. Their parting was amicable, but the proposed venture as now outlined was obviously not satisfactory to either man.

Carlson's $250,000 of seed capital would have given McManus a cushy beginning (extra money to fall back on if needed), but Jim felt that, if absolutely necessary, he could make do with $75,000. He had only $25,000. Yet, borrowing $50,000 without collateral is a trick few men can achieve. In this instance, Jim was very, very lucky. No collateral was required, and he was obliged to pay, believe it or not, only the prime rate, because the lender turned out to be his brother-in-law, Robert Nicolet.

Nicolet had made a bundle in the air-freight industry. He retired in 1970 and, unusual as it may seem (he was only thirty), decided to move to Florida and keep himself busy playing golf. All the brother-in-law jokes I'd ever heard conditioned me to think of them as incompetent sad sacks, but this Nicolet turned out to be the proverbial "friend in need [who] is a friend indeed." He agreed to lend Jim the $50,000 at terms that were really too generous. As it turned out, McManus paid him back in full within seven months. (Nicolet later tired of his early retirement and became president of MCA's real-estate division.)

The idea that started Jim's gold rush had first occurred to him while still at Glendinning. This was the time when S & H Green Stamps had become a way of life for America's housewives. Supermarkets gave customers green stamps with each purchase, and the green stamps were redeemed for household goods at S & H Redemption Centers. Marketers estimated that 80 percent of the U.S. population collected Green Stamps, or similar coupons.

S & H Redemption Centers carried almost everything for the home, and Jim had the thought that the redemption centers would be the perfect place to test consumer opinion of new products. This was McManus's idea and he had been working out the kinks while he was still at Glendinning. However, he had not yet made any move; it was all theory. He explained it to Ralph this way: "I have been working on this with the S & H Green Stamps company in mind, and it is now just about ready to go. But it hasn't gone anywhere yet. We have no signed contracts, and I have no consumer-product contracts. Now I can either leave it at Glendinning and it would die, because there is nobody here to promote it—the fire is in *my* chest—or I can steal it, and you wouldn't know the difference, or I can buy it. I don't want to leave it at Glendinning to die, and I don't want to steal it."

The upshot was that Jim and Ralph settled on a price of $75,000, payable over three years.

McManus put it to S & H this way, "Here is how you can make additional profits in your redemption centers—lease me a small space for a product-testing booth." They reached an agreement and Jim set up his booths where he would be sure of positively qualified consumers. McManus staffed the booths with young marketing researchers who gave out samples of new products from consumer-product corporations, products such as cold medicines, dog food, cat food, cigarettes. If a person had a dog, he would receive a sample of dog food. If he was a smoker, he would receive a sample carton of cigarettes. If he suffered from allergies, he would receive a sample of a new over-the-counter medication, etc. Sampling an *entire* population was expensive and inefficient. In contrast, *selective* sampling was efficient and considerably less expensive.

Basically, Jim's young researchers would qualify potential participants by determining who might benefit from the variety of products being offered. In exchange, the participant would give the researcher his or her name and address so the product company could later conduct its own marketing research as to consumer satisfaction with the product, current brands used, satisfaction with package design, and with this information in hand the company could then project a demand for the new product. At the end of a three-year period, McManus had twenty-two of the largest consumer-product corporations participating in his selective sampling in S & H Redemption Centers.

In those three years, MCA did over $3 million in business, profiting nearly $1 million.

By the end of 1975, however, Jim's brilliantly conceived business was finished. Housewives now preferred buying products sold at the new *discount* centers. So, supermarkets and gas stations stopped giving away trading stamps, and switched instead to discounting. Happenstance!

By this time, quite a few of Jim's clients had become true believers in his marketing abilities, and several had suggested that he come up with a method for inexpensively distributing coupons to consumers. It was one of his top executives, Dan Pratt, who had the new idea for MCA's innovative coupon program. Entire pages of free-standing, full-color inserts on magazine stock were bought up by MCA (at wholesale, in effect), then small advertising spaces were sold to consumer-product manufacturers at "retail." The coupons making up the free-standing inserts offered consumers ten to twenty-five cents off the products being advertised to induce the consumer to try a new product, or to revitalize sales for a tried and true product, or possibly to prevent new competition from eroding an existing product's market share.

Consumers began to look to these brilliantly colored, glossy coupon pages as avidly as they had formerly looked for their S & H stamps. Subsequently, another division of MCA offered pages with similar savings, but these black and white coupons appeared in the main body of the newspaper as opposed to a free-standing insert.

MCA's new newspaper co-op couponing program received discounts for (1) Frequency—advertising at least one day a week in 1,000 newspapers around the country; (2) Volume—free-standing inserts of ten to twenty pages for those same 1,000 newspapers every week; and (3) Cash—an accounting system ensuring prompt payment to take advantage of discounts offered by newspapers for advertisers who prepaid their advertising or paid within ten days.

While these discounts are available to any major advertiser, few can afford the frequency or volume of advertising that MCA did, or the cash flow to handle prepayment for 1,000 newspapers weekly. The idea caught on quickly, and it, too, was soon making money, really big money.

Several clients then said, "You do this promotion business so well, why don't you help us with our advertising?"—after which one of Jim's clients helped him buy an already very successful advertising agency, Ally & Gargano.

Ally & Gargano clients included Federal Express, Saab, and Dunkin' Donuts, among others. Jim realized that the world did not need yet another advertising agency, but he surveyed the competition and concluded that MCA could do a better job because his people were motivated, creative, and experienced marketers with the best possible background.

Later on, Jim said, "My basic idea was simply to become, in effect, the Hertz Rent-A-Marketing Brain for corporate America." Frankly, that did not sound like that much of an idea to me, but I did my best to put my own prejudices aside.

"We set outselves up as a premier think tank in marketing and sales promotion for consumer packaged goods. Our very special idea was putting a number on how different people react to different stimuli: advertising campaigns, package design, different products, different brand names. Then by using those numbers from product to product, we could more easily evaluate the effectiveness of the campaigns that were being considered. The numbers could also obviously be used to tell our clients how and why consumers behave as they do."

MCA, acting as consultants to corporations, had two advantages over the corporations' in-house talent. First, MCA was not on the corporate payroll, being paid *only* for selected projects. Second, its consultants benefited from the experience gained in the variety of projects in which they had participated, whereas the corporation's in-house marketing staff runs the risk of boredom from constant exposure to the same product lines.

Then, because he had been so successful with his initial marketing ideas, clients came to Jim for the additional services that subsequently became reasons for starting all those new companies, and finally even encouraging MCA to buy several not-so-related businesses.

McManus believes that religion and economics make the world go round. He did not plan to make any contributions to business through religion, so he has made a continuing study of economics. In the twenties and thirties, financial people were the driving force behind business. In the forties, the war years, industrial and engineering specialists were the driving force. That era lasted into the fifties, when marketing became the driving force behind most of the business equations, mainly because of television and mass distribution: supermarkets and discounters. Jim's company came into being during this marketing-development period. His company and his clients profited from this upsurge. MCA was doing what other marketers were doing, but as Jim said, "We were doing it better."

One night, McManus was watching his employees file into the elevator and suddenly realized he was watching his "inventory" walking out the door. So to add "brick and mortar" to his thriving business, Jim rounded out his investment portfolio by diversifying; he acquired a chain of restaurants, a computer company, a regional airline, real estate, and, finally, a venture-capital partnership.

I said, "Jim, it's suicidal to move into such highly competitive areas." McManus just smiled and said, "We're striving to deliver a better consumer value in a highly competitive, highly segmented market with products that are frequently used, and we can do it comfortably because 'our edge is better people.' "

I said to Jim, "For the most part, I have not been able to attract better people, and I know that we pay above the market. How can you attract them?"

"That's easy. I pay them better. Our unique compensation package attracts and retains superior people." This gave Jim a chance to spell out one of his axioms: "Power to the people."

To ensure the success of his various enterprises, McManus knew that he was totally dependent upon hiring good people and keeping them. So he prepared a liberal and unusual profit-sharing and incentive plan. He calls it "margin management."

"You know, Mortimer, the greatest disservice that the Harvard Business School has ever done to the corporate world is dreaming up the concept of management by objective—the five-year plan, the idea that you can say your revenues will grow X percent in the next five years and your profits will grow 20 percent, etc. Why control a company's growth by limiting your expectations on its rate of growth?'' Jim believes in planning a company's growth on an annual or even semiannual basis, using currently available market information.

At MCA, each divisional president is responsible for bringing in his division on the goal he projects for himself. A preestablished profit margin is agreed upon between Jim and the president: usually 15 or 20 percent, depending on the business—a risky business might aim for a slightly higher return than a stable business. That percentage is skimmed off the gross income (similar to a royalty) and returned to the parent corporation as a reserve, perhaps, to help an ailing division, or a fund with which to start a new division. "I have seen too many service businesses distribute all their profits, returning nothing to the pot. Yet a service business *must* invest time and hard-earned dollars to deliver a better product. Service companies must invest in themselves."

Margin management was not an altogether altruistic idea, but it turned out to be a bonanza for almost everyone, including, of course, MCA. Most important, it took a huge management burden off Jim's back, that of controlling expenses. Each president was totally responsible for making a profit, so he became the one who carefully watched the expenses—*all* the expenses. And, naturally, so did his executives. They all worked together to make certain there was a profit, and, obviously, the bigger the profit the better, because they were all sharing. When compared to the way it was before the concept of margin management, it's easy to see why Jim was, shall we say, having a ball.

The following is an example of how one MCA division would distribute profits, assuming gross income of $10 million with the preestablished goal of a 15 percent profit:

| | |
|---|---|
| Revenue | $10,000,000 |
| Operating Expenses | 7,500,000 |
| Gross Profit | 2,500,000 |
| 15% of Gross Revenue to MCA | 1,500,000 |
| | |
| Profit-sharing Trust | 300,000 |
| Bonuses Paid Out | 700,000 |

Assuming $10 million in gross revenue, $1.5 million will go directly to the parent corporation. Part of the money will be used to increase the corporation's shareholder equity, and part of it will be used as seed money for new companies, or to aid companies that might be ailing. From the $1 million remaining, 15 percent of all eligible employees' salaries in the division ($300,000) will be set aside for a profit-sharing trust, and the balance ($700,000) will be paid out in bonuses to participating executives in the division.

Jim's revolutionary modification is that instead of the parent corporation receiving the remainder of a division's profits after operating expenses, salaries, bonuses, and taxes are paid, he earmarks 15 percent of gross sales and leaves the balance for the individual division president to budget. Jim thinks this makes for responsible fiscal management, as well as being a major tool for motivation.

As an extra plus, all employees are instantly vested in pension and profit-sharing plans. In addition, management employees are allowed to participate in real-estate-development ventures so that they can share in the (hoped for) profits.

Jim owns 51 percent of the outstanding stock, and the balance is owned by the company employees. There is only one restriction: employees who leave *must* sell their stock back to the corporation.

When McManus described his incentive system, I could not help thinking that it might be slightly futuristic. But

Jim is waiting for it to be proven so *consistently* successful that it will qualify for use as a case study at the Kellogg Graduate School of Management, his alma mater, at North-western University.

The venture-capital division came into being because clients were understandably curious about the many divisions MCA had started, as well as the success of the various businesses they had acquired. MCA had the smell of success. Clients and friends asked to invest money in future businesses. Encouraged by all this interest, Jim set up the new investment division known as MarketCorp Ventures. Investors were limited to investing $1 to $5 million, none higher. And *only* corporate money, no individuals. Within a short period of time, MarketCorp Ventures raised $66 million. At this writing, $20 million of the total has been invested, and that $20 million investment has increased in value from 1984 to $36 million in 1986. Not bad.

"So far, we've invested twenty million of the sixty-six million dollars in fourteen investments, and already we know that five are turkeys, four look to be big winners, and five are just in between. . . . Our fund keeps looking for market-driven ideas. When we find one, we fund it. I expect we'll have a thirty-percent-plus compounded annual rate of return when it's finished, which means our sixty-six million dollars should be worth four hundred million in seven years. We'll take our 20 percent as a fee [the usual venture-capital fee], which is $80 million. Then we'll be happy, go home, and probably start another fund."

I asked Jim about those MCA companies that didn't work out, the ones on which, perhaps, he too "lost his shirt." Jim said: "No, they don't always work out. We started twenty-six businesses; twelve were successful, twelve failed, and two are still being evaluated. Most of them were started with our 'sandbox money,' the fifteen percent of our gross profit we set aside every year as a development reserve. That's the money we use to develop information about ideas we think might be productive. If things look good, we give an idea a try. If it isn't working after twelve months, we kill it."

Now comes the big question: If four out of five new businesses fail, why should McManus do any better? Jim's answer is quite persuasive. "Well, for starters, most businesses are started by people who lack our collective experiences. We not only have our personal experiences, but because we are professional marketing specialists, we also have the experience of all those companies we have worked with. We have the experiences resulting from the millions of dollars of clients' money that was spent on research. So when we start a new venture, we do have an edge, an angle, and we have been, as you can see, quite successful. And even though we may have hit some clinkers, they are far outweighed by the successes, and the proof is visible in the continuously increasing value of our bottom line."

Let me conclude this chapter with the "Ten Commandments" Jim McManus has developed over the years for helping to ensure the success of his—and perhaps your—new business ventures:

1. With whom is more important than where.
2. The more you give, the more you get.
3. Make a commitment to the development of new products.
4. Put product before profits.
5. You have permission to fail.
6. Spend money to make money.
7. Insist on individual accountability and authority.
8. Everybody profits.
9. Be the best.
10. *Have fun.*

# 16

■ □ ■

# WILLIAM RAVEIS
## Scratch an Entrepreneur
## and You Will Find an Ego

The case of thirty-nine-year-old Bill Raveis, real-estate entrepreneur, stopped me cold because in my opinion he had no sound reason for starting his own business. Yet if he continues to go the way he has been, he will wind up as one of the country's biggest brokers.

I met Raveis for the first time one Sunday afternoon in early October. Bill had been working in his garden. He was dressed in cowboy boots, blue jeans, and a plaid shirt over a navy blue T-shirt. He did not exactly look like a well-heeled, brilliantly successful entrepreneur.

I have frequently pointed out to aspiring businessmen that an executive should project the image of an executive whether he is in the garden, in the office, at a dinner party, or at a convention. At the same time, I know only too well that the substance of a man—his ability and his motivation—is much more important than the image he projects.

WILLIAM RAVEIS, *founder and CEO, William Raveis Real Estate*

Substance was what I found as I delved into Bill's background.

Raveis graduated from the University of Dayton in Ohio with a B.S. degree in business administration and went to work for Sikorsky Aircraft. The company paid for his postgraduate work in the nascent field of computers. Subsequently, he was offered a job at Westinghouse, where he had responsibility for a research project that kept him busy for three and a half years. His boss and his boss's boss were thrilled with what he had produced, a completely new computer program. His program was introduced at an international symposium of the Westinghouse big brass, and Bill was invited to attend. The chairman introduced Bill's new system with considerable fanfare, and the president of international operations expounded on its usefulness. They were all proud of the role they had played, but they never once introduced Bill Raveis as its creator, nor, indeed, did they even mention his name.

Scratch a true entrepreneur and you will find an ego. It is hard to understand the Westinghouse chairman's lack of sensitivity. He had not climbed the ladder by being tactless. Yet the snub was real, at least as far as Bill Raveis was concerned. His feelings were deeply hurt, and he vowed never again to work for anyone else.

Raveis was twenty-seven, without a master's degree. He was already making $28,000 a year. In 1974, it was the income of a young man on the rise. Bill spent six months looking around at various possibilities. He decided to go into the real-estate business, even though he had no previous experience. There were several factors that influenced him:

1. He and his wife Barbara had recently bought a new house for some $30,000. The real-estate agent collected

a commission of $1,800 for which, in Bill's opinion, the agent had done practically nothing. To Raveis, it looked like easy money.

2. To open a real-estate office required only miniscule capital.

3. The competition, in his mind, was almost nonexistent. Agents, at that time, worked for bosses who had no business disciplines, no computer knowledge, no understanding of the way a business should be run. To Raveis, they all seemed to be mom-and-pop operations. To put it another way, Bill was confident that he had a better business sense. He knew too that he was completely willing to work extra hard to make himself a success.

Raveis opened Yankee Realty in a $60-a-month, one-room walk-up, with a telephone, a desk, and a chair. His income plummeted from $28,000 to zero, allowing for the fact that his wife Barbara took a job as a part-time teacher at $250 a month.

It's interesting to note here that Stew Leonard opened his business with the name Clover Farms Dairy and switched to Stew Leonard's. Raveis opened with the name Yankee Realty and at the first taste of success changed the name to William Raveis Real Estate. It was an impossible name to pronounce, so he capitalized on it in his advertising—"Pronounced Rave-is." Unlike Leonard and Raveis, I lacked the courage to change the name The Custom Shop (which I dislike) to David London, Shirtmaker. That's what I had wanted to do, and what I should have done.

Raveis and I did have one thing in common: neither of us was content with our imminent futures and gambled to change them. As I see it, however, I had a good idea and the necessary capital to start my business. Bill had nothing but the real-estate broker's license he earned by going to Fairfield University at night.

Now just between us, don't you agree that Raveis should have held on to his job while he explored the real-estate business part-time (either at night or on weekends)? Or at the very least, shouldn't he have first taken a job working for someone in real estate to get a little experience so that he could formulate a realistic *modus operandi*? On the other hand, I expect you have met couples of whom you said, "He married her?!" or "How did *he* ever hook such an attractive wife?" To put it another way, two and two does not always equal four.

Let's see what happened. Right away, the real-estate business proved to be much more difficult than Raveis had anticipated. Although he was a newly licensed broker, he was not accepted by the local real-estate board. Any real estate that was up for sale was distributed to all members of the local board, but to become a member, one had to open a commercial office after having had at least one year of experience.

Poor Bill had no access and very little business. In 1974, he spent $2,000 on advertising and had a net income of $6,000. In 1975, he spent $15,000 on advertising (dipping into his savings and his wife's earnings) to earn $9,000. In 1976, he spent $30,000 on advertising for a net income of $30,000. No one ever said that opening your own business was easy.

But Raveis had the quality necessary to endure the slow start-up. I asked, "Why, Bill, should customers go to you instead of where they had been accustomed to going?" His answer included these four points:

1. "My inner strength. I knew I would offer better services than other companies."

2. "I was willing to work harder and longer, and did, in fact. In the beginning, I advertised myself as the 'after dinner agency service—service in the comfort of your own home.' No need to come to my office, etcetera."

3. "My marketing approach was different. All agents advertised property that was for sale: 'Cape Cod, 3 BR, 1 1/2 acre,' 'Colonial 3 yrs old. Sacrifice sale,' etc. I never advertised that way. I advertised my agency: 'Fastest-growing agency in Connecticut,' 'Sold in 3 days'—a whole series of ads that hammered away at achievement."

4. With one small office and two, three, four, and later five telephones, he could hire real-estate salespersons as independent contractors—no obligations for large overhead. Independent contractors were not entitled to any salary or drawing accounts. It was all straight commission.

In 1976, Bill opened a second office and continued to advertise himself and his agency. Today he has twenty-two offices in Connecticut, with representation in over ninety towns. In 1984, his advertising budget alone was $2.5 million. You may draw your own conclusions as to his current income.

His biggest break came in his fourth year, because that is when he found a real angle. His was the first agency to advertise a corporate relocation service at no charge. This was the period when large corporations from all over the country were opening headquarters and/or branches in Connecticut. Bill had first shot at those "displaced executives" who were forced to relocate to Connecticut, by offering them a free consultation service. There was no obligation to buy or rent from him or through him. But as his company had the first contact, they did make most of the sales.

In his fifth year, Bill put his computer knowledge to good use, and this was his second angle and the one that brought him his biggest growth. His was the first real-estate agency to use computers (initially at great expense—in excess of $1 million) to great advantage. A customer would say, "I want to spend ninety thousand dollars; I need four bedrooms, and I want my children to attend school in Fairfield or Westport." Raveis would press a button and, presto, show the customer immediately what was available. And this service was immediately available at all twenty-two of his branches.

But Bill didn't stop there either. He opened his own mortgage company, his own insurance agency, and is now doing his own banking. In other words, Raveis is a one-stop real-estate miniconglomerate—no partners, no stockholders, no franchises.

In 1981, the bottom fell out of the real-estate market in Connecticut, and his net income plummeted to $35,000. But his rebound was even faster, and today he is number one in the state. And he started only twelve years ago with literally nothing—no capital and no real-estate experience!

Subsequent to this interview, I concluded a real-estate deal with Bill. I owned a newly built 43,000-square-foot enclosed shopping center in Brookfield, Connecticut. I had been obliged to take it over when my tenant (the original builder) defaulted. It had been badly mismanaged and was losing money. Bill offered to buy it from me. I wasn't present at the negotiations—they were handled by Tony Bergamo. But Bill's offer was so skillfully planned that I could see, at first hand, why he had become successful. Raveis has more than energy. He also has the brains and the imagination one needs to have achieved so much in so little time.

AL HAM, *founder and owner, "The Music of Your Life," pictured here with Liza Minnelli.*

# 17
∎ ◻ ∎

## AL HAM
## A Musician's Virtuoso
## Venture into Radio
## Programming

Al Ham's success with a syndicated radio program called "The Music of Your Life" is no more or less unusual than the success achieved by the other entrepreneurs I've met. However, there is an enormous difference in the business setting. Ham, aided by his attractive wife, Tamara, operates in Huntington, Connecticut, from a quiet cottage in the woods—a pastoral paradise seemingly far removed from the world of commerce.

Al is a soft-spoken, gray-haired, slightly overweight, gentle man. He is sixty-two, but one might guess that he is in his mid-fifties. He is a musician and has been devoted to music all his life.

Ham attended Amherst College, majoring in music, but never earned a degree. He started his own performing career on the guitar and eventually became a professional bassist during the big-band era. As with many talented instrumentalists, he dabbled in writing and arranging, and the bands provided an excellent means of getting his arrangements played.

Much later, he did the writing, scoring, and conducting of musical themes for television programs around the country. Those themes are really the musical logos that serve as instant identification for a variety of programs and promotional pieces. His earnings from all those positioning themes resulted in a steady continuous income.

In 1972, Al served as a line producer on the made-for-TV film *Give 'Em Hell, Harry,* a profile of Harry Truman starring James Whitmore. It was this successful experience that kindled Al's desire to produce his own radio program.

The big-band sound had virtually disappeared from the air waves, having been pushed aside by Elvis Presley and the Beatles. Even William B. Williams's famous "Make-Believe Ballroom" on WNEW in New York City had to be homogenized in order to reach the market of eighteen-to-forty-nine-year-olds, the age group most attractive to advertisers.

Al's concept was quite simple. He knew that there was a large older audience who could no longer find the music they were raised on. He thought that if he could use existing recordings and by means of new electronic breakthroughs "clean up" the music by eliminating the nicks, scratches, and hisses so noticeable on early albums, he could offer radio audiences a familiar but new-sounding sound. He personalized his concept with the name "The Music of Your Life." I thought the name was more than a little awkward.

But then he had a further idea which, to my mind, was the major reason for his success. Ham persuaded many of the original recording artists to tape testimonials plugging the new format, and they agreed to do it without being paid. They were only too happy to cooperate, knowing that the success of Al's new format would result in a resurgence of their own careers. So at least once every hour, Rosemary Clooney—or Tony Bennett, Johnny Mathis, Peggy Lee, Benny Goodman, Frank Sinatra, or some other artist—would say, "This is Rosemary Clooney, and I thank you for making the music of my life the music of your life."

Having been in the music business for so many years, Al knew many of the stars personally, and it was relatively easy for him to get their cooperation, often with only a phone call. The presence of all those stars gave his programs both credibility and status. The listeners, all fans, enjoyed being addressed directly by these well-known, talented stars.

But how did Ham actually get his program on the air? It happened this way. While attending a conference of radio station executives, Ham met a programmer from a station in Bridgeport, Connecticut, who bitterly complained that his station was not doing well. The station was owned by Art McLynch. Ham talked about his new programming idea, and an appointment was arranged. McLynch's main business was a modest-sized heavy-construction company. He had taken a little fling on the side into radio. Unlike many flings, it did not have a happy ending. McLynch's partner in the station was a dentist from Newark, and they were losing money. That's why McLynch was receptive when Al came along with his idea.

Ham's proposal, roughly stated, went like this: Al, McLynch, and the dentist would be partners in a business syndicating "The Music of Your Life." They would use the Bridgeport station, WDJZ, as a pilot to prove that their program could resuscitate an ailing station. If the pilot was successful, the rest would be easy. McLynch and the dentist would take care of the development costs and invest a modest $30,000 into the marketing of the project. For their investment, they would receive 50 percent of the profit; Al would receive 50 percent for his contribution as artistic director and developer. The station format was to be 100 percent "The Music of Your Life" programming.

Ham moved from New York City to Connecticut, where he spent a year accumulating the original recordings and cleaning them up electronically. Ham then started putting the tapes together for programs to be run on WDJZ. As tapes were completed, they were aired. It took him a full year to get the needed number of tapes finished so that their station could run his programs exclusively.

The Arbitron ratings of station WDJZ went from an immeasurable rating to a rating of 6.5, meaning the station became profitable. Based on those results, a second station, owned by Bob Lappin in Springfield, Massachusetts, signed on. Al served as a musical consultant, giving the Springfield station the musical schedules to follow and scripts for the local announcers.

Ham could have provided a ready-to-air tape that would have the music complete with "canned" introductions by his own announcer. But he found that the stations needed more flexibility and wanted to use their local announcers to provide a really necessary local personality.

Eventually, the programming tapes evolved into three categories, progressively more sophisticated (and more expensive):

1. *Matched-flow Reel-to-Reel.* Nine times a year, a station receives four tapes, ready to be aired, cut into segments of five to seven songs with openings indicated for introductions to the pieces, plus prerecorded promos. By inserting a variety of "interruptions" (news, commercials) after songs, and by varying when the interruptions are played, the station can disguise the repetition so that its listeners do not easily discern that

"Moonlight Serenade" is always followed by "I Left My Heart in San Francisco."

2. ***Segments Randomly Selected:*** For example, four tape machines are used, each with a five-to-seven-song sequence (as above), and the machines play their segments in a random order. You might have, say, selection number one from machine one, selection number one from machine three, selection numbers one and two from machine two, selection numbers one and two from machine four, selection number two from machine three, etc., etc.

3. ***Random Selection by Individual Song.*** Tapes are transferred onto cards, and Al provides a programming schedule indicating the optimum number of plays for each song (novelty songs should not be played as often as old standards) and the time of day when each song would be most enthusiastically received. Al understood his markets and knew that commuters turning on the radio to and from work demanded different programs than housebound listeners. With this approach, Al could provide two and a half weeks of listening with *no* repetition.

It is difficult to pin down the actual product being offered to the radio stations. Certainly, the tapes and promotional plugs are a salable product. But what is really being sold is Ham's contributions as a media and programming consultant.

Subscription prices vary from $600 to $5,000 per month, depending on market size and program selected. He currently has 180 clients. After his first client sale, Al bought out his partners, and today, like me, he has no partners. Unlike me, he wants no one else to participate in the management or direction of his company.

As with our other successful entrepreneurs, he has marketed his idea well, and maintains complete control. Early on, he set up the credit arrangements to be strictly cash, no bartering. Once the initial client station was established, Al moved out of the procurement and selling areas and hired specialists in both fields.

Ham also understood that his main competition was and is packaged beautiful-music programs. And that competition is fierce. Seemingly, almost anyone who can put together a few tapes can go into the business. But the "Music of Your Life" program is one of a kind, because it is the only one that uses the original recording artists to plug the programs regularly—every day, every hour.

You should see him in his work place. A tiny cottage, deep in the woods, incredibly quiet. There is only his wife, Tamara, and a secretary in an outside room. Ham projects the image of a priest who is happy with his pope and his congregation. But beneath the peaceful picture is a shrewd and successful entrepreneur.

# 18

### ■ □ ■

# ED MITCHELL
# A Retail Clothier Brings in
# the Crowds with a Warm
# Family Touch

E d Mitchell, a college dropout, walked out of an active
business career at the age of fifty-three because he was
tired of being home only on weekends. Ed had been a consultant, and it is the nature of a consultant to spend the
week wherever the clients are, and they are inevitably out
of town. So one day, out of the blue, really, Mitchell decided
to open a business in his hometown of Westport, Connecticut—meaning that he could even go home for lunch if he
chose to.

Let's take a close look at Ed's background and qualifi-
cations to see if there was any logical reason for quitting
his work as a management consultant to become an independent retail clothier.

Back in 1937 (the year I opened my first Custom Shop),
Mitchell formed a partnership with Russell Allen, an engineer with considerable experience in making time and

Bill (the golfer) and Jack (the tennis player) Mitchell in their latest Burberrys sportswear.

## Great companions: as comfortable with Burberrys style... As they make you feel with Ed Mitchell's service!

On a typical Saturday, Ed Mitchell's of Westport is full of good customers from New Canaan, Wilton and other nearby enclaves. Often they strike up a conversation with co-owners Bill and Jack — usually about some of our 4,000 suits, 7,000 pairs of shoes or maybe something new that just came in.

Lately a lot of the talk has been about Burberrys new spring sportswear. The terrific selection. The bright warm weather colors. To quote Bill, "The new Burberrys collection is fabulous" (except that Bill is very likely to repeat the word "fabulous" more than once). To get an idea of the kind of clothes you can expect to find at Ed Mitchell's — take a good look at the Ox Ridge horse show crowd. Then come on in. As for the service — Bill has a word for it.

Good to see y
Ed Mitch
OF WESTPOR

670 Post Road East, 227-5165.    Store Hours: Mon. — Wed., 9:30am-6pm, Thurs. — Fri., 9:30am-9pm, Sat., 9am-6pm.

BILL *and* JACK MITCHELL, *Ed's sons, now run Ed Mitchell, Inc. (from a typical family-oriented Ed Mitchell newspaper advertisement)*

motion studies to increase productivity of industrial workers. Both men then had the idea of taking the time and
motion concept out of the factory and putting it into retailing. They achieved a modest degree of success, and after
many good years sold their business to Grey Advertising,
one of the country's largest agencies.

Ed was a deacon in his church, and along with Norma,
his wife, had always been active in community affairs.
Norma was also a Sunday School teacher, and their two
sons, Jack and Bill, following their parents' lead, were both
active in scouting and in sports. The whole family was
people-oriented; they entertained frequently, and Ed, of
course, was service-oriented as well.

Mitchell had now spent some twenty years as a consultant showing retailers how to run their stores more effi-
ciently. His decision to open his own clothing store in
Westport sprang from a very personal need—like my skinny
neck and Julian Brodie's elderly family. When Ed took his
two sons shopping for clothes, he found there was no suit-
able store in town. He had to take them to the nearest large
city, Stamford, some twenty miles away. Then and there
he decided that Westport needed its own store with young
men's clothing. He was only partly right.

Ed had enjoyed a close relationship as a consultant with
Cluett, Peabody, maker of Arrow shirts, and Schoeneman,
a leading manufacturer of medium-to-better-priced men's
clothing. As both manufacturers gave him promises of support, his idea of opening his own store seemed to be sure-
fire. And it would be close to home.

Armed with his business experience and the support of
two major suppliers, Ed opened a clothing store for young
men, stocked with slacks, blazers, sport jackets, sport shirts,
sweaters, some shirts, some ties, two suits (a gray flannel
and a navy blue), but mostly sportswear. He intended to

cater to young men the age of his two sons (at this time Jack was a college freshman and Bill a high-school sophomore). It took him only a week to realize that young men shopped with their fathers, who often wore the same styles as their sons. Ed quickly decided to add men's clothing. It was the same thinking that prompted him finally to add women's clothing fifteen years later—mothers and wives frequently accompanied both sons and husbands.

So in 1958, at the age of fifty-three, the age at which many men feel themselves to be over the hill, and in some instances almost unemployable, Mitchell started his own business.

It was tiny—900 square feet. I cannot say it was ugly, but it surely was not inviting. I remember looking in the door and saying to myself, "He'll be out of business in a year or two." But Ed had two things going for him that I didn't know about. One was his wide acquaintance with his fellow townsmen. "Our first customers were our friends, and the business was built on service, not product." Second was his ability to make people feel welcome, a quality which he and Norma passed on to their sons and subsequently to their staff. That family feeling is best exemplified by his advertising. And because of his experience at Grey Advertising, he felt well qualified to use advertising advantageously.

Ed wasn't selling clothes, he was selling a service, and it paid off handsomely. Today his store is known throughout Fairfield County and most of neighboring Westchester County in New York. His business has grown from the 900-square-foot store to a 25,000-square-foot facility (he is now building an additional 7,000 feet) carrying a complete line of clothing for both men and women, from a $69,000 business that first year to over $12 million in 1985—big sales for a town with a population of only 28,000.

A complete line of name-brand and designer clothing are

his staples—names that have long been household words, like Arrow, Hathaway, Polo, Bally, Ferragamo, Southwick, Hickey Freeman, Jockey, and Burlington for the men; Liz Claiborne, Perry Ellis, and Pendleton for women. All clothing includes a free alteration service from a staff of over twenty tailors. (Free alterations for women are an "angle." Women's alterations are always an extra charge elsewhere.) Freshly brewed coffee, lollipops, soft drinks, and snacks are set out for customers and their families. An oversized television screen entertains children and sports fans, and customers enjoy visiting with Ed and his sons. Ed Mitchell's store is like a club where one is very apt to meet a friend or neighbor.

There has been only one small crisis in Mitchell's sustained growth. Once a trusted employee embezzled a substantial sum. This stab in the back was distressing, but not fatal, and Ed decided not to prosecute and ruin the embezzler's life—he put another mortgage on the house and went on.

Mitchell is fortunate to have two sons who are capable, bright, interesting men, both already involved in Fairfield County's civic affairs. Although Ed does keep his hand in, he has, for all practical purposes, turned the ownership and operation of the business over to Bill and Jack. That was done some ten years ago, and the continued growth in the past decade is a testimonial to the ability of the younger Mitchells.

What can we learn from all this? Only that twenty-five years ago, starting with an idea conceived on impulse, never properly researched, executed with a commitment to friendly service plus (and a big plus) a bold use of advertising, Mitchell built New England's largest clothing store. He had five very small angles. One was his ability to welcome people as friends, and, acting as role models, he, his wife, and subsequently their two sons, passed this elusive quality on to all their 135 employees. Second, his advertising dominated the second page of the local biweekly newspaper, and frequently featured the family. Third, he carried only name-brand quality merchandise, getting the full benefit of the brands' national advertising. His suppliers all participated in the cost of the local advertising. Fourth, he offered *free* alterations, a really important (and costly) plus. Fifth, as the area benefited enormously from the exodus of many of New York's largest corporations, so did Ed Mitchell, obtaining more than his share of customers from among the new, mostly affluent, residents.

This enormous suburban growth also brought in some formidable competition. In 1983, Alfred Taubman, the king of shopping-mall developers, opened an AAA-1 enclosed mall in Stamford. He called it Town Center. Good name, and very successful too. It may take another year or two to determine whether or not that new center will have any negative effect on Ed's business. So far, it hasn't. But even if it should, the income to the entire family will still be far beyond Ed's wildest dreams, with a future that makes me look like a pretty bad picker, but only because I didn't know personally the man behind the name.

# 19

∎ □ ∎

# GEORGE LINDEMANN
## Filling an Old Prescription
## in a Lucrative New Way

E arly each June, the George Lindemann family moves
into their castle, beautifully situated on ten acres of
waterfront property in Greenwich, Connecticut. They have
a view of Long Island Sound that is unsurpassed. In the
winter, they live in their Sutton Place town house in Manhattan, where their perfectly groomed lawn borders directly
on the East River. The house was formerly owned by Ar-
istotle Onassis. Yet when the Lindemanns bought it, they
did a complete renovation, a reconstruction job inside and
out that went on for two years. Winter weekends find the
family aboard the Lindemann jet, flying to Florida, where
they stay at their villa on the grounds of the Palm Beach
Polo and Country Club. And to this we must add their
thirty-meter yacht that they now keep in the Caribbean.

The Lindemann family is close-knit. All three children
have been indulged, relentlessly, yet there is no indication

GEORGE LINDEMANN, *founder and chairman of the board, Metro Mobile CTS, Inc.*

of their having been spoiled. And each one seems to have acquired the tradition of phoning home every night from wherever he or she might be.

George's wife, Frayda, has her Ph.D. in musicology. Adam, the eldest son, is a polo player and former playboy, now a graduate of Yale Law School; George Jr. is a recent graduate of Brown and a world-champion horseman; and Sloan, the youngest, who, fortunately, inherited her mother's beauty, is now a junior at Brown, and like her brothers, rides in competition.

George Jr. makes competition riding a full-time career, which means entering riding meets all around the world. His horses are shipped by plane. It also means that some member of the family (if not the entire family) is usually present to cheer him on. On several occasions, "Georgie" has represented the United States in international competitions. The Lindemanns own about forty horses, three of which are world champions. During the summer, the horses usually spend time on the thirty-four-acre farm that Lindemann bought when the large Rosenstiehl estate in Greenwich was broken up. The entire family works hard and plays hard.

There are usually contradictory elements in the make-up of any successful person, and fifty-year-old George Lindemann is no exception. Despite his seemingly total involvement in business, his life is actually centered around his family.

Lindemann was an impetuous young man. He married Frayda when he was twenty-three, the age at which most of today's young men are breaking up with their second live-in girlfriend. Yet he projects a conservative image. He is well spoken, articulate—frequently dogmatic—but on the whole quite reserved. I assumed he was the type of person who would visit his doctor regularly, and was surprised to realize he has an almost reckless disregard for his own health, especially for a man with such close family ties. He is not only a chain-smoker of cigars, he actually inhales each puff.

Is George Lindemann's current affluence the result of an inheritance like the Rockefellers? Or was he just plain lucky? The answer is neither. George Lindemann really earned his money the old-fashioned way. There were three consecutive, enormously successful business ventures, but in this book we'll talk only about the first, because George's entrepreneurial talents are so easily visible in that first venture, a pharmaceutical company named Smith, Miller & Patch.

George Lindemann graduated from the Wharton School with a B.S. in finance, despite the fact that he was an impossible student, cutting as many classes as he attended. But he did have an early aptitude for business. At the age of thirteen, he began reading the balance sheets of businesses being offered for sale that his father brought home from the office for his own nighttime study. Lindemann Sr. was the majority stockholder and chief executive officer of a successful business dealing in inexpensive cosmetics.

George was still a junior at Wharton in 1957 when he recommended that his father diversify his cosmetics business by moving into pharmaceuticals. George suggested a company—Carroll, Dunham, Smith—which his father then actually bought.

I asked him why he chose that particular company since it was going downhill at the time. George replied, "Mortimer—Carroll, Dunham, Smith did well during the forties, the war years. When I wanted to acquire it, the company was headed by the founder's grandson. Under *his* management, they launched an expansion program at the wrong time—by building a 200,000-square-foot manufacturing plant in New Jersey—just before their business took a serious and unforeseen downturn.

"But I liked the field, and certain reading I had done led me to believe that the pharmaceutical business in general had to continue growing. Dad bought the company based on its liquidation value. He paid nothing for good will. I wanted to buy it because I felt that under my management it could enjoy a vigorous growth."

Even at that early age, George displayed the self-confidence of a born entrepreneur.

George was still at school when his father bought a second pharmaceutical company, E. S. Miller Laboratories (annual sales of $300,000, specializing in injectable medication). He then bought a third pharmaceutical company, E. L. Patch (annual sales of $800,000), with the mainstay of its product line a laxative, Kondremul. Patch's plant was in Stoneham, Massachusetts. Mr. Lindemann's idea was to cut back overhead by bringing production for all three of the acquired companies to Carroll, Dunham, Smith's underutilized plant in New Jersey, after which he could sell off all the surplus equipment.

There were now three pharmaceutical divisions, three presidents, three research and development departments, and three sales forces. The companies were consolidated and a new corporation was formed named Smith, Miller & Patch (thereby losing whatever good will the individual corporate names carried). The first year as a consolidated operation produced sales of $1.25 million, and sales decreased by 10 percent each of the following two years.

In 1960, Lindemann Sr. fired the last of the presidents and presented the company to his son. George was twenty-four and he had a company to run, but no products of any consequence. The products he did have were in highly competitive areas. George said, "I decided to search out a specialty field that the major manufacturers were not interested in developing. I had a choice—not large to be sure, but there was a choice: dermatology, proctology, urology, ophthalmology. I selected ophthalmology." The entire research and selection process took about three weeks.

In studying the field, Lindemann searched for an angle. He learned that Alcon Laboratories, the largest pharmaceutical company specializing in ophthalmological products, was successfully packaging eye medication in plastic squeeze bottles. In the past, they had always been packaged in glass bottles with separate eye droppers. Another company, Alergan, packaged steroids (antiinflammatory compounds) in plastic bottles. George continued: "There was the angle I needed. I only had to find medications that were still being packaged the old way, in glass." Ciba, a large manufacturer selling mainly to distribution houses, had three products that filled the bill: an antihistamine, a decongestant, and a decongestant with an antihistamine.

The first product George introduced was a decongestant that had been on the market for many years. "All I did was change the glass to plastic, reduce the size to half, triple the price, and make it a prescription drug." I asked him why anyone would want to buy such a product.

When George responded, there was a twinkle in his eye. "Let's take a hypothetical case. A patient complains about irritated eyes. The doctor knows that a decongestant will handle it—call it a placebo effect, but the eye will look better and the patient will feel better. The doctor takes time to discuss the problem. Then he writes out a prescription.

"How does that patient feel when he goes to the pharmacy, gives the druggist the prescription, watches the druggist reach over the counter, blow some dust off a box, and hand him some medication for $1.99—after he just paid $50 for a visit to his ophthalmologist! Might he be miffed? Yes, and understandably so.

"This way, he gets a prescription filled and doesn't know what's in the bottle. Result: The patient is happy, the druggist is happy because he makes more money, and I am *especially* happy for all of them."

After three years, that product was—and is to this day— the largest-selling decongestant on the market. George expanded the line further by duplicating other ophthalmological products that could be put into plastic squeeze bottles. Then he renamed each one. The result was spectacular. However, beyond the packaging and products, George discovered something even more essential to his success—and that was his personal marketing style.

George decided that in addition to his advantageous packaging, he needed something more. So he created the superdeluxe cocktail party. He entertained lavishly at every state, regional, and national meeting of ophthalmological groups, always presenting the finest, establishing a hallmark of quality and excellence.

Second, he produced films on innovative surgical procedures, creating a surgical-film library that was to become a major teaching tool within the profession. When I asked how teaching fitted into his strategy, he explained that at most medical-association meetings and symposia, the same doctors stood at the podium and delivered the same papers. After several meetings, the papers became rather dull.

"Showing innovative surgical techniques on film was interesting, but even more important, it encouraged the viewers," George said. "Each doctor thought he could perform that operation or at least give it a try. Also, the films generated good will because they were made by professionals and doctors with ongoing practices ... and as the films were shown throughout the country, the participants' names were publicized." He added: "With good editing and enough cases, everyone could be a great surgeon"—and indeed everyone was.

"Jose Baracar was a well-known ophthalmologist from Barcelona, Spain. I selected Baracar as an ophthalmologist whose work would be recorded because he was already famous, and he was not from the United States, so there was no risk of alienating American ophthalmologists. I hosted an annual luncheon at which each doctor who had participated in the films would receive a handsome plaque and be photographed while receiving his award. The award was later hung in the doctor's office, adding to his prestige and thereby increasing the patients' confidence."

Now that he had finally found his niche, Lindemann's obsessive motivation carried him forward to attain an almost professorial position. He followed, in considerable detail, the research that was being performed throughout the world in the field of ophthalmology. He studied medical journals and papers to keep abreast of advances, so that his conversations with doctors reflected far more than chitchat. He could—and did—project the image of a well-rounded, knowledgeable colleague, and this added even more prestige to the products that emerged from his company.

In addition to earning substantial profits, George played an important role in advancing several ophthalmological procedures. He explained, "Because I befriended Fyodorov, a well-known Russian ophthalmologist, my company was the first in the United States to sterilize implants for cataract operations." One of George's close friends from college, Dr. Miles Galin, also became involved in implants and was responsible for successful research on the subject. Neither Miles nor George wanted to profit from the results of their combined efforts, and they contributed the entire research project to the medical profession. Today the cataract-implant business grosses some $400 million annually. It was the commercialization of the implant concept that later brought to market the first permanent-wear soft contact lens: Permalens.

In 1970, just ten years after Lindemann Sr. had bought a floundering company for his son, gross sales reached $16 million annually. George sold Smith, Miller & Patch to Cooper Labs for a cool $60 million.

What you have just finished reading is not the whole Lindemann story, it is only the beginning. There are two additional installments that I am not including because my main emphasis throughout this book has been on how successful businesses get started, and describing the personalities involved.

George went into the cable-television business in 1971 and built the sixteenth largest cable company in the United States. He sold it in 1982 for the highest price then ever recorded for such a company. He almost immediately formed a new company called Metro Mobile at a time when cellular telephones were still a dream. As of this writing, the venture is enormously successful, encompassing nationwide cellular-telephone systems with an over-the-counter market value of almost $1 billion, and he had only just turned fifty.

JULEE ROSSO (left) and SHEILA LUKINS, *cofounders and owners,
The Silver Palate*

# 20

## JULEE ROSSO and SHEILA LUKINS
### Gourmet Takeout, Palatable at Any Price

J ulee Rosso and Sheila Lukins are cofounders and sole owners of The Silver Palate, a $10 million gourmet food business that started, as so often happens, from humble beginnings. Since Julee handles the public relations for the firm, the story of their entrepreneurial success is told from her point of view. But obviously it has been a partnership in which Sheila is equal, and equal to the task.

Julee, now in her early forties, was born in Kalamazoo, Michigan. She earned a B.A. degree with a triple major in French, education, and history. Her professional career started in New York in fashion, public relations, and advertising. "In my first twelve years, I was fortunate to have been employed by three of the largest textile firms in the country—Bancroft, Monsanto, and Burlington—either as fashion director or as the in-house advertising director." For starters, Julee had a lot on the ball. She was good to look at, easy to talk to, and easy to like. Her forte was fashion.

I asked her how it came about that she and Sheila started The Silver Palate. Like the businesses of many other entrepreneurs, it was the result of a *personal* need. As a career woman, Julee had been working long hours, so there was precious little time to cook at home. Although she enjoyed cooking, she resented spending her Saturdays (those when she was not at the office) in the kitchen and thought there should be an alternative. She enjoyed entertaining, but it had become increasingly difficult, and she did not like the idea of calling in a caterer every time she gave a small dinner party. She thought there should be another way and cast about for an alternative. She assumed that other working women and all those newly divorced men were in the same boat. "It occurred to me that there would be an immediate market for a small shop that would offer the kind of well-prepared food on a takeout basis that anyone would be proud to serve guests."

In July 1977, while still at Monsanto, Julee gave a party celebrating Oleg Cassini's new line of Monsanto sheets and used Sheila Lukins as the caterer. Sheila was a graduate of the Cordon Bleu School in London. She enjoyed working and entertaining. She was already married and the mother of two young, active daughters. At the time, she had a tiny business of her own, with a big name, The Other Woman Catering Company—"So discreet, so delicious, and I deliver." Her business was directed primarily to New York bachelors who found it difficult to entertain at home without a "little woman in the kitchen."

Sheila's menu for the Cassini breakfast party included a delightful, innovative berry mousse on croissants—pretty bizarre fare for 1976. Julee was intrigued and impressed with Sheila's creative breakfast menu and broached the idea of a takeout gourmet food business. Sheila was reluctant at first (there were those two little children and her own small catering business), but after giving it some thought, decided to try it; she thought she could handle it, because it would still be part-time.

So I asked Julee, "What's so special about opening a place with takeout food? Everyone does it." Julee said: "Oh, no! Quite the opposite. We were first. Back then, there was nobody else, and in any case there certainly was no food as good as ours. Our only competition was Zabar's, which specialized in Germanic food, Jewish delicacies, really, and Barney Greengrass, who offered mainly bagels and an assortment of salmon."

The gourmet food that Julee and Sheila offered was of a completely different style and quality. Sheila had been trained as a gourmet cook, and Julee was just one of those naturally good cooks who enjoyed cooking and collecting recipes.

Julee had actually resigned her corporate position in 1976 to open her own business as a consultant in marketing, publicity, and sales promotions for the fashion industry. Julee really thought of their contemplated business as a part-time hobby.

First on the agenda was selection of a site for their store. Madison Avenue was their first choice, but rents were much too high. They settled for a hole in the wall (156 square feet) on Columbus Avenue where their rent would be a modest $500 a month. They spent $21,000 in renovations, including the refrigeration. Julee's first idea had been to call the store The Best of New York, because she had thought to *buy* her favorite dishes, dishes that she had discovered in the various restaurants she and friends had patronized. (Not at all a good idea because her prices would have been much too high.) Now, with a partner in the kitchen, the entrées could be prepared by Sheila and brought to the store each day. Breads, appetizers, salads, and desserts could be brought in from the outside.

Florence Fabricant, a long-time friend, wanted to include them in a feature she was doing on the renaissance of Columbus Avenue for *New York* magazine, and she was up against a deadline. The partners had not been able to decide on a name, although they had come up with about thirty suggestions. Florence suggested The Silver Palate, out of nowhere, really. Maybe she was thinking of the phrase "born with a silver spoon in his mouth." The partners said, "Done—let's do it."

In 1977, Columbus Avenue had not been discovered by anyone but The Silver Palate, O'Neal's, and the Museum Café. They were lucky because Columbus Avenue would soon become one of New York City's most fashionable areas.

As Julee was telling me this story, I thought to myself, "How can you just open a store with food that is perishable and expect to sell it out to the last piece? Because what you don't sell, you throw out." It seemed like an almost impossible merchandising problem. But Julee's promotional experience turned out to be equal to the task.

During the renovation period, Julee ran a chocolate-chip cookie contest to determine who could bake the best chocolate-chip cookies in the neighborhood. Local children, along with Julee and Sheila, would be the judges. So The Silver Palate was widely discussed even before it opened. The entire neighborhood knew, almost at once, what was going on and when the opening was scheduled. That was the day the winner would be announced.

By a coincidence, the day of the opening was the same day Central Park was having a major concert, a free concert performed by the New York Philharmonic, which drew an audience of some 75,000. Concertgoers traditionally pack a picnic to eat while listening to the concert, and these concertgoers bought out everything The Silver Palate had to offer.

The food was great, and the shop's reputation spread quickly. In addition to their takeout food, the women began a catering service for large dinner parties and cocktail parties. This gave them an additional edge. Whenever they catered a party, they would increase the volume just enough to put those dishes into the store inventory. This enabled them to offer a larger variety of entrées and salads.

Their prepared food sold well, but their "shelf food," the condiments, sauces, salad dressings, jams, etc., mostly imported, moved slowly. Julee and Sheila were not at all enthusiastic about those products, so they set about preparing their own. Their first products included beautifully prepared cherries, damson plums, Seckel pears, apples, and other fruits, preserved in brandy or spiced white wine sauces and displayed in unique jars.

Julee's public-relations experience was responsible for two early breaks. The first was having alerted the neighborhood of their arrival with the cookie contest. And the second came about when Patricia Wells, food editor at the *New York Times*, wrote an article on how nicely European food products were packaged, some having the lids covered by pretty fabric secured with a colored rubber band. Julee wrote Patricia Wells a complimentary letter on the article and suggested that she see for herself what was new on Columbus Avenue, namely The Silver Palate.

Patricia wrote a short piece on the shop in the *Times*, and their business literally doubled from that moment on. "It really took off," Julee said, and the business continued to grow. The momentum never stopped.

The Silver Palate was still in its infancy, and the company was succeeding beyond their most extravagent dreams. Part of that, of course, was their foresight, or luck, in having selected Columbus Avenue as their site.

In 1978, Bob Suslow, the new president of Saks Fifth Avenue, and Gordon Segal, who owns and operates Crate & Barrel, a mail-order gourmet catalogue business and retail chain, were both shopping Columbus Avenue to see what all the excitement was about. They were charmed by The Silver Palate, and also by Julee and Sheila. They struck up a deal. Saks and Crate & Barrel would put The Silver Palate's preserved goods in their Christmas catalogues and in the gourmet sections of their various stores.

The retail price of $30 to $40 for one jar was certainly high, but not beyond the reach of affluent Saks customers. The canned fruits made unique gifts, not only because of their content, but because the women had found a European source for canning jars of unusual design and decorative enough to be used as vases after they were emptied.

The success with Saks and Crate & Barrel sent a signal to Julee's fertile brain: establish a wholesale business for their own brand. There was no way they could create a market through advertising, because they lacked that kind of money. If success was to be enjoyed, it had to come through publicity. They developed a successful procedure for obtaining editorial mention. They simply scheduled periodic luncheons in their homes for various food editors.

Julee and Sheila built good will in another way. They gave out recipes of even their very best-selling dishes. That in itself generated considerable word of mouth by customers and the press.

At one luncheon party in 1981, Barbara Plum of *Vogue* magazine picked up one of Julee's in-house newsletters that were being mailed regularly to the four hundred retailers selling their merchandise. Barbara said, "You know, you girls ought to write a cookbook."

And that's what they did in the summer of 1981. They prepared the recipes, and Sheila, who is not only a gourmet cook but a graphic artist as well, did illustrations for a collection of quotes gathered by Julee.

"The purpose of the first cookbook was to lend credibility to our food line. The irony was that we sold a couple of million cookbooks." An interesting point: theirs was the first American cookbook to be translated into French and sold in French bookstores. That, of course, was a real coup.

Initially, cookbook sales were slow. Then, by word of mouth, sales built, slowly at first, then rapidly. The recipes were easy to prepare (very important), recipes that most readers were able to execute successfully. A grilled piece of chicken or fish became a delectable meal when marinated in or topped with one of The Silver Palate's mustards, sauces, splashes, chutneys, or savories.

A business contains within itself a dynamic force, and once it is in operation, "outside things" can and sometimes do happen. Too often, of course, things happen that have an adverse effect. But in this instance, the cookbook turned out to be a time bomb and The Silver Palate's business exploded.

Their fame has spread as far away as Tokyo. The Japanese people have developed an appetite for Western-style gourmet cuisine, and The Silver Palate opened two retail outlets in Tokyo in 1986, outlets that also included their first restaurants.

I am skipping the story of how Julee and Sheila went about finding contractors to make their food, how they found the right person to handle administration, etc., because these are problems common to all businesses. The thing that is not common is the successful execution of an idea because of the entrepreneur's aptitudes, because of happenstance, and in some cases, in spite of happenstance.

One small aside. Julee and Sheila elected not to use a distributor, meaning the prices they charged could be 20 percent less than they would have been otherwise. They used telemarketing to keep in touch with their now 2,000 retailers.

Their business success and, of course, all that profit, was terribly exciting and worth the long hours and the many lost weekends but the business turned out to be fun for another reason. They would have an idea and produce it within a week. Then they could get an immediate reaction from their clientele. From this point of view, it has become a continually fun-filled enterprise for them.

Perhaps it is time to bring this story to an end, and say merely that they now gross about $10 million a year. They are no longer working seven days and seven nights each week, and they have even reached the stage where they can enjoy entire weekends away from their business.

And that does it for my case studies. So now, let's move on to the nitty gritty. Once you have decided on your idea, and have decided to go into business, you generally need to raise capital. There are various ways that this can be done. You'll find them in the next chapter, along with ways to protect your idea.

# 21
. ▫ .

# How to Raise Capital—
# How to Protect Your
# New Idea

In an earlier chapter, I suggested that prior to embarking on your entrepreneurial journey you should ask yourself the question *Why should anyone buy this product or service from me instead of where he or she buys it now?* If you answered that question substantively, you might have come to the conclusion that your venture's success was virtually guaranteed. In reality, there will be unexpected problems, in the beginning, and continuing throughout your company's existence. Previous chapters indicate a variety of problems that might possibly be circumvented.

In addition, there are two basic problems that immediately face almost all new venture start-ups: how to raise the necessary capital, and how to protect your new idea. Let me sketch in some ways to handle those problems.

## START-UP CAPITAL

There are a variety of sources of start-up capital for you to consider:

*Wealthy Individuals.*   This would be my preference. Go to these "angels" directly. You can usually get a referral from your banker, lawyer, or accountant.

As a potential investor, I would not put up my money if an entrepreneur were unwilling to risk some of his own. That, for me, would be a determining factor. In addition, he would present an idea that had an "angle" that I liked; be a person I considered to be of a serious nature; and be willing to play an active part in the management of the new venture.

*Venture Capitalists.*   You can find these institutional risk-takers through venture-capital association directories. They usually prefer companies that have a strong potential for going public or being acquired, and they typically look for an annualized rate of return on their investment of 40 to 60 percent for five to seven years.

*Small Business Administration.*   The SBA has a variety of loan programs for small businesses that are unable to borrow money from banks.

Most SBA loans are made by private lenders and guaranteed by the SBA. Currently, the SBA will guarantee up to 90 percent of a loan, with a maximum guarantee of $500,000. Maximum allowable interest rates (2 1/4 to 2 3/4 percent above prime) are set by the SBA. A business owner must have been turned down for a conventional loan by a private lender before becoming eligible for an SBA loan.

The SBA makes a small number of direct loans of up to $150,000 each. These generally have slightly lower interest rates than regular commercial loans. Call your local SBA office (look in the government listings of your phone book) for information on loan programs.

***Sbics and Mesbics.*** Small-business investment companies and minority-enterprise small-business investment companies are privately owned and operated companies licensed by the SBA to provide loans to small firms. Investment amounts vary from under $100,000 to over $1 million. They also offer management assistance. Call your local SBA office for a list of SBICs and MESBICs.

***Commercial Banks.*** Banks generally require security and guarantees before making start-up loans and sometimes impose other restrictions on the borrower. You can expect to pay the prime rate plus one to four points.

***Business Development Corporations.*** BDCs are privately owned corporations chartered by many states to make loans to small businesses. They are flexible lenders and can often come up with a creative package that would be unavailable from more conventional sources. They can generally make loans guaranteed by the SBA.

***State Venture-Capital Funds.*** More than twenty states have programs providing venture-capital funds for small businesses, particularly start-ups. Requirements vary greatly from state to state. Contact your banker or your state or local economic or industrial development office to see whether your area has these or other capital-funds programs for which you might be eligible.

***Public and Private Stock Offerings.*** Stock offerings require experienced legal help, as they must conform to the federal securities laws and the state blue-sky laws. There are several brokerage houses that specialize in small offerings.

If you want to borrow money, you must have a business plan. There is no easy way to write a business plan, because each business plan has to be individually custom-made. Before you're done, you'll wind up talking to everyone you can find with expertise in your field, and you'll probably become good friends with your local research librarian.

You will do better to write the plan yourself, because experienced investors quickly spot plans done by outsiders. Financial projections that come out of a canned computer program are also a turnoff.

According to Joseph Mancuso, director of the Center for Entrepreneurial Management in New York and author of several books on writing business plans, potential investors spend an average of five minutes screening a plan. If you don't grab their interest from the beginning with the executive summary, your plan will probably disappear into the waste basket. Here are some sources to guide you in writing an effective business plan:

> *How to Write a Winning Business Plan* by Joseph R. Mancuso (Prentice Hall).
>
> *Business Plans That Win $$$* by Stanley Rich and David Gumpert (Harper & Row).
>
> *Business Plan for Retailers* (Management Aid No. 2.020) and *Business Plan for Small Service Firms* (Management Aid No. 2.022), available free from the Small Business Administration, P. O. Box 15434, Fort Worth, Texas 76119.

## EVALUATION AND PROTECTION OF A NEW PRODUCT

Obviously, you should research the market carefully to see if your idea is already out there. But in addition you might also want to have your product rated at an evaluation center, for example at the Wisconsin Innovation Service Center at the University of Wisconsin at Whitewater. They rate new products on thirty-three different criteria. The charge is only $100, and you will get a detailed report. It really is a bargain.

The Wisconsin Innovation Service Center is not the only one; there are others. If you would rather stay close to home, phone Wisconsin and they will give you the name of a local service.

Unfortunately, there is no guarantee of confidentiality, so it's important to keep a record of your creative procedures—a dated log, you might say. And it might not be a bad idea to discuss your idea with a lawyer. There are "invention brokers" who sometimes work on a contingency fee.

Write to the Small Business Administration, P. O. Box 15434, Fort Worth, Texas 76119, for the Small Business Bibliography, No. 91, *Ideas into Dollars*. It is free and it tells you all about the creative process and how to protect your invention.

Several forms of legal protection are available. The one you use depends on what you have created.

## Patents

A patent will give you the right to stop others from making, using, or selling your idea in the United States for a specified time. Unfortunately, it takes about two years for a patent to be approved.

A utility patent is the most difficult and expensive to get. It is available for such things as a new and useful process, method, or machine, or for an earlier manufactured article. You won't get the patent if a patent examiner decides that your idea would be obvious to a person having ordinary skill in the technological area of your invention.

A design patent covers a new, original, and ornamental design for the appearance of a manufactured item. The rules are basically the same as for utility patents, but design patents are generally easier to get and cheaper. They may not turn out to be of much value, because someone else can easily make your item with a slight change in the design without infringing on your patent.

The basic filing fees for individuals and small businesses are modest—less than $300. You must also pay periodic maintenance fees totaling $1,400 for utility patents.

If you are thinking of getting a patent, better get yourself a patent lawyer. The Superintendent of Documents, Washington, D.C. 20402, will send you a list of attorneys or agents registered with the Patent and Trademark Office (PTO).

A search to check for conflicts with other patents can run $300, sometimes more. Legal fees of $2,500 to $3,500 for obtaining a utility patent aren't unusual; fees for complex inventions can be even higher. If you draft the application yourself and then have your lawyer refine it, your fees will be much lower. A book that might be helpful is Calvin MacCracken's *Handbook for Inventors* (Scribners).

You can get a free half-hour consultation with a patent attorney in your area through the American Intellectual Property Law Association's Inventor Consultation Service. That should be enough time to discuss your invention and whether you should take steps to protect it. The application form is included in *How to Protect and Benefit from Your Ideas*, available from the AIPLA, Suite 203, 2001 Jefferson Davis Highway, Arlington, Virginia 22202.

There are things you can do to protect your idea even before you apply for a utility patent. Keep comprehensive daily work notes as you develop your idea and have them witnessed by at least one person you trust who understands the invention but who is not involved in the invention process. Also establish the date of your invention. The old trick of mailing yourself a registered letter describing your invention and keeping it unopened does not help. The fact that it bears a postmark makes no difference. Instead, you should prepare an invention disclosure describing your invention and have it read and signed by two trustworthy outsiders who understand what you're doing. If necessary, their testimony can establish conception at least as early as the date they signed the disclosure. In addition, you can send a signed disclosure to the PTO under the Disclosure Document Program. The PTO preserves the disclosure for two years in secrecy, but the program isn't a substitute for your own records or for filing a patent application. (Filing automatically establishes a date of invention.)

You don't have to wait for the issuance of the formal patent to begin marketing your invention. Once you've filed the application, you can put "Patent Pending" on your product. It doesn't give you any legal protection, but it is a strong deterrent to potential infringers.

For more information, get a free copy of Management Aid No. 6005, *Introduction to Patents*, from the Small Business Administration, P. O. Box 15434, Fort Worth, Texas 76119, or from your local SBA office. The booklet *General Information Concerning Patents* and information on the Disclosure Document Program are available free from the Commissioner of Patents and Trademarks, Patent and Trademark Office, Washington, D.C. 20231.

## Copyrights

A copyright protects original "writings" against unfair copying for the life of the author plus fifty years. If two or more people collaborate, the copyright is good for fifty years after the death of the last survivor. If the work is done for hire or under a pseudonym, protection lasts seventy-five years from publication or a hundred years from creation, whichever is shorter. Covered works include poems, books, articles, paintings, sculpture, musical compositions, lyrics, maps, and pictorial designs, such as the printed material on board games. A copyright protects only the way an idea is expressed, not the idea itself.

For more information, write to the Register of Copyrights, Library of Congress, Washington, D.C. 20559. Ask for Copyright Kit 118, available free.

### Trademarks

Names, symbols, labels, slogans, or any other mark or device (such as a soft-drink bottle) used to identify goods and distinguish them from those manufactured or sold by another can be registered as trademarks. A service mark is the same thing for services. You gain federal trademark and service-mark rights only when the marks are actually used in the sale of goods and services in federally regulated commerce, such as interstate commerce.

It is a good idea to have a patent lawyer do a "clearance search" even before you begin to use a mark to be sure it isn't already in use. There's a filing fee of $175 for registration with the PTO. That protects your mark for twenty years, and you may renew every twenty years. For more information and registration forms, request a free copy of the booklet *General Information Concerning Trademarks,* from the Commissioner of Patents and Trademarks, Patent and Trademark Office, Washington, D.C. 20231.

## CORPORATE STRUCTURE

It has been traditional when starting a business to form what is called a "C" corporation, the advantage being that you could not be sued personally for the company's debts. While with this your home, automobile, and personal bank account were never at risk, you paid in another way because the corporation paid a tax on its profits. For example, in 1985, a New York corporation might be paying 58 percent of its profits in taxes: 48 percent to the federal government and about 10 percent to city and state.

A few years ago, the government approved an "S" corporation structure. Should you form an "S" corporation, you would have the same personal protection against creditors as with a "C" corporation, but you would not pay corporate taxes. All profits generated by an "S" corporation would be treated as your personal income. In today's tax structure, this should be a decided advantage. However, do not make your decision without discussing it with an attorney or an accountant who specializes in taxes.

## WHAT IS YOUR ENTREPRENEURIAL QUOTIENT?

The Northwestern Mutual Life Insurance Company of Milwaukee, Wisconsin, prepared a series of questions that might help you determine your own E.Q. (Entrepreneurial Quotient). While I am not suggesting that you take this test too seriously, I think under the circumstances you might find it interesting or, at the very least, amusing.

Do you ever wonder if you could succeed as an entrepreneur? Studies of successful entrepreneurs reveal common characteristics—family background, early experiences, motivations, personality traits and behavior, values and beliefs. How do you fit these patterns? What is your Entrepreneurial Quotient, your E.Q.?

This test can't predict your success—it can only give you an idea whether you will have a head start or a handicap to work with. Entrepreneurial skills can be learned. The test is intended to help you see how you compare with others who have been successful entrepreneurs and to help you consider whether you really want to work at building your own enterprise.

Here goes . . . add or subtract from your score as you play to learn: "What's Your E.Q.?"

1. Significantly high numbers of entrepreneurs are children of first-generation Americans. If your parents were immigrants, score plus 1. If not, score minus 1.

2. Successful entrepreneurs were not, as a rule, top achievers in school. If you were a top student, subtract 4. If not, add 4.

3. Entrepreneurs were not especially enthusiastic about participating in group activities in school. If you enjoyed group activities—clubs, team sports, double dates—subtract 1. If not, add 1.

4. Studies of entrepreneurs show that, as youngsters, they often preferred to be alone. Did you prefer to be alone as a youngster? Yes = plus 1. No = minus 1.

5. Those who started enterprises during childhood—lemonade stands, family newspapers, greeting-card sales—or ran for elected office at school can add 2 because enterprise can usually be traced to an early age. Those who didn't initiate enterprises, subtract 2.

6. Stubbornness as a child seems to translate into determination to do things one's own way—a hallmark of proven entrepreneurs. If you were a stubborn child (you wanted to learn the hard way), add 1. If not, subtract 1.

7. Caution may involve an unwillingness to take risks, a

handicap for those embarking on previously uncharted territory. Were you cautious as a youngster? Yes = minus 4. No = plus 4.

8. If you were daring, add 4 more.

9. Entrepreneurs often speak of having the faith to pursue different paths despite the opinions of others. If the opinions of others matter a lot to you, subtract 1. If not, add 1.

10. Being tired of a daily routine is often a precipitating factor in an entrepreneur's decision to start an enterprise. If an important motivation for starting your own enterprise would be changing your daily routine, add 2. If not, subtract 2.

11. If you really enjoy work, are you willing to work overnight? Yes = plus 2. No = minus 6.

12. If you would be willing to work "as long as it takes" with little or no sleep to finish a job, add 4 more.

13. Entrepreneurs generally enjoy their activity so much that they move from one project to another—nonstop. When you complete a project successfully, do you immediately start another? Yes = plus 2. No = minus 2.

14. Successful entrepreneurs are willing to use their savings at the outset of a project. If you would be willing to spend your savings to start a business, add 2. If not, subtract 2.

15. If you would be willing to borrow from others too, add 2 more. If not, subtract 2.

16. If your business fails, will you immediately work to start another? Yes = plus 4. No = minus 4.

17. If you would immediately start looking for a well-paying job, subtract 1 more.

18. Do you believe entrepreneurs are "risky"? Yes = minus 2. No = plus 2.

19. Many entrepreneurs put long-term and short-term goals in writing. If you do, add 1. If you don't, subtract 1.

20. Handling cash flow can be critical to entrepreneurial success. If you believe you have more knowledge and experience with cash flow than most people, add 2. If not, subtract 2.

21. Entrepreneurial personalities seem to be easily bored. If you are easily bored, add 2. If not, subtract 2.

22. Optimism can fuel the drive to press for success in uncharted waters. If you're an optimist, add 2. Pessimists, subtract 2.

*A score of +35 or more:*
You have everything going for you. You ought to achieve spectacular entrepreneurial success (barring acts of God or other variables beyond your control).

*A score of +15 to +35:*
Your background, skills and talents give you excellent chances for success in your own business. You should go far.

*A score of 0 to +15:*
You have a head start of ability and/or experience in running a business, and ought to be successful in opening an enterprise of your own if you apply yourself and learn the necessary skills to make it happen.

*A score of 0 to −15:*
You might be able to make a go of it if you ventured on your own, but you would have to work extra hard to compensate for a lack of built-in advantages and skills that give others a "leg up" in beginning their own businesses.

*A score of −15 to −43:*

Your talents probably lie elsewhere. You ought to consider whether building your own business is what you really want to do, because you may find yourself swimming against the tide if you make the attempt. Another work arrangement— working for a company or for someone else, or developing a career in a profession or an area of technical expertise—may be far more congenial to you, and allow you to enjoy a lifestyle appropriate to your abilities and interests.

*Provided courtesy of Northwestern Mutual Life Insurance Company, Milwaukee, Wisconsin.*

# 22
■ □ ■

# Conclusion:
# Do You Still Have
# Your Shirt?

Having read this book, you have, I hope, learned some worthwhile things about starting your own business. At the very least, you know that four out of five new enterprises fail, meaning that should you consider starting your own business you will do it despite the fact that the odds are against you. When I started The Custom Shop, for example, I did not know that—nor did I know how to raise capital. Fortunately, I didn't need to. But if it had been necessary for me to raise $10,000 in 1937, I would not have known how to go about it. In fact, knowing that I am not a borrower, I am quite sure that I would *not* have opened that first Custom Shop.

You also have a fairly detailed review of how seventeen successful entrepreneurs built their own businesses, despite the unexpected problems they encountered. In my case, the unexpected problem was the continuous raiding of my best people by others who wanted to start a competing chain. I have not spelled out how very often it happened, but it has been going on continuously for almost fifty years.

And you have undoubtedly been persuaded by now that total concentration is called for, and from the variety of new ideas that has been explored, you may also have reached the conclusion that the possibilities are indeed endless. If your idea is good enough, you will certainly take customers away from their usual source, because in one way or another you will be giving more without charging more.

Each entrepreneur takes his or her own unique path to success. But there are several generalizations that you should not overlook:

**1.** Your basic concept must be sound; and in order to determine that it is indeed sound, a fair amount of research should be done to make sure that your angle is unique.

**2.** Never underestimate the fact that there is and always will be a lot of competition out there. The more successful you are, the larger the number of people who will try to do what you are doing and perhaps do it even better. Some of your potential competitors will be brilliant, and most of them will be hardworking.

**3.** It's hard to assess the extent to which ego, self-confidence, and drive enter into the make-up of an entrepreneur. Most of my entrepreneurs started out with considerable self-confidence, and frequently an entrepreneur has to push on dauntlessly with what he believes in. I am thinking of my refusal to sell out to Seligson, and my continuing demand that it is our obligation and duty to teach our customers the necessary practice of color coordination, despite the fact that the customer is not usually cooperative. I am thinking of Imperatore's relentless drive for business at a time when business was so hard to come by, or the way men like Mike Weatherly, Gene Ballin, Bill Raveis, and Joe Kohler kept pushing—their footsteps never faltered.

Imperatore is an example of what can be accomplished

with obsessive behavior. Joe Kohler is an example of giving a new twist to an old idea, as is Stew Leonard, who took milk-processing out of the factory and into his retail store. Dean Sloane realized that ten doctors, working together, could produce revenue through an activity impossible for a doctor working alone (and at the same time provide a much-needed service). Glenn Bernbaum recognized (among other things) the cash value of snob appeal. Jim McManus realized that the marketing expertise he had acquired at Procter & Gamble and at Glendinning could be applied to many completely different businesses. George Lindemann "just knew" there was money to be made in pharmaceuticals. After buying his company, he dug around, looking for an opening. Once he found the opening, he applied his own brand of marketing with the obsessive energy of an Imperatore.

**4.** And on the positive side, think of this. Once you are in the game as a player, new opportunities will come your way, things that would not happen if you had not set out as an independent entrepreneur. For example, it is unlikely *The Silver Palate Cookbook*, which alone has earned the authors tons of money, would have sold so well, or even been published, if Sheila and Julee had not become "players" in their business.

**5.** Happenstance too is certain to play a part. The Korean War and a long strike served to demolish two of Gene Ballin's most promising real-estate developments. Mike Weatherly's lumber venture in Honduras was knocked out of the box by a military coup. Kenneth Lane's business was so strong because of a surge in jewel thefts—which meant that fashion leaders were afraid to venture out wearing their real diamonds, so they publicized the fact that they were wearing fake jewelry, and fake became fashionable.

The significance of the happenstance factor can be seen

immediately in the twists and turns some of my own investments have taken over the years.

In 1962, I bought 550 acres of gently rolling land overlooking the Pacific in San Mateo County, twenty-one miles south of San Francisco. It was zoned for five-acre parcels and situated between two north-south throughways (one that had been recently built) plus an east-west throughway that was being built. I picked up the property on the low side because a friend's option was running out. Then came happenstance. One year after I bought the property, the county changed the zoning from five acres to a hundred acres. (I could build only one home on a hundred acres.) Then the county ran out of funding to complete the east-west throughway—it was to have hit a corner of my property. Result: I have been sitting on this land for twenty-five years losing income on my $1.3 million purchase price. Fortunately, the taxes were taken care of by the rent I received from the farmer who lived on my land. (We are now in court contesting the zoning change that, in effect, amounted to confiscation without reimbursement. I could not sue earlier because other similar cases had lost. But in 1987 the California Supreme Court handed down a landmark decision that now makes it possible to sue. Anyway, I have joined with my neighbors along the coast in a class-action suit.)

In contrast, a few years later I was part of a small group that bought a sixty-five-acre airport in Armonk, New York. It cost us $5,000 an acre. Three years later, IBM put up a huge installation on the adjoining land. The following year, the state needed fourteen of our acres to build a new throughway. By court order, the fourteen acres were condemned at $125,000 an acre—thank you, IBM.

Two more examples. I bought a small building on New York's Fifth Avenue at Fifty-sixth Street for $325,000. It was 1953, and it housed what was to be The Custom Shop's flagship store and our executive headquarters. Thirty years later, I sold that building for $9 million. No brains, just happenstance. On the other hand, in 1965, I bought the DePinna Building at the corner of Fifth Avenue and Fifty-second Street. It was an unlisted distress sale that I came across through a friend, Eric Javits, nephew of the late senator. DePinna, a longtime carriage-trade specialty store, had four years left on its lease. Wanting to replace the building with a new one, I took the Minskoff brothers in as junior partners because of their long expertise in building and developing real estate in the metropolitan area. The projected new building required considerable zoning variances before we could proceed with the construction. The Minskoffs dallied too long, and it was late 1971 before we were fully cleared. By that time, the bottom had fallen out of the New York real-estate market. I bought the building for $5.5 million and sold it to the shah of Iran for $8.6 million. But nine years later, the land under the DePinna Building would have been worth $25 million. It was the late shah who then put up the building we had planned. As of this writing, it is estimated to be worth about $60 million.

The enormous increase in the value of New York real estate was the result of political uncertainty abroad, which fueled the flight of capital to the United States from oil-rich Arabs, the Japanese, English, French, Germans, and even Argentinians and Mexicans. At the same time, a rush from the city to the suburbs had been precipitated by a rise in crime and the deterioration of New York's public school system. This migration, specifically of corporations and their top executives, helped to underwrite the phenomenal success of Ed Mitchell, Bill Raveis, and Stew Leonard. In Raveis's case, it was especially important because of the free relocation service he offered to the many executives who were being transferred to Connecticut, not only from New York City but from Texas and other parts of the country. So much for happenstance.

I knew none of these factors nor had I any such far-reaching perspective when I started my own business. I too was lucky in a sense because I started my business in 1937, a Depression year, and benefited from the fact that business in general (and my business in particular) continued to improve as a result of World War II.

The use to which you put the various ideas you have just read about might very well affect the outcome of your new business. And to those of you who decide to go ahead, good luck—hopefully, you will be the one entrepreneur who makes it, while the other four cry themselves to sleep. And to those of you who decide to keep your shirt by *not* going ahead, congratulations; you are undoubtedly making the right decision.

As I said in the beginning, endless trouble is the price we all must pay for the gift of life. The best way to handle those troubles, I have found, is to relax and face the situation and do what needs to be done. The troubles won't disappear, but you can handle them with less anguish, knowing that you are not alone—that everyone else is having, or will be getting, their share. It is not a question of "if"—only a question of "when."

So there you have it; and by all means, no matter what, remember to keep smiling.